PROJECT CENSORED'S

STATE OF THE FREE PRESS 2024

The Top Censored Stories and Media Analysis of 2022–23

EDITED BY **Andy Lee Roth** AND **Mickey Huff**
WITH **Project Censored**

FOREWORD BY **Alan MacLeod**

ILLUSTRATED BY **Anson Stevens-Bollen**

THE CENSORED
— PRESS —

Fair Oaks, CA • New York

A JOINT PRODUCTION OF THE CENSORED PRESS
AND SEVEN STORIES PRESS

The Censored Press
PO Box 1177
Fair Oaks, CA 95628
censoredpress.org

Seven Stories Press
140 Watts Street
New York, NY 10013
sevenstories.com

ISBN 978-1-64421-332-2 (paperback)
ISBN 978-1-64421-333-9 (electronic)
ISSN 1074-5998

College professors and high school and middle school teachers
may order free examination copies of Seven Stories Press titles.
Visit https://www.sevenstories.com/pg/resources-academics
or email academic@sevenstories.com.

9 8 7 6 5 4 3 2 1

Printed in the USA

Book design by Jon Gilbert

DEDICATION

To Daniel Ellsberg
April 7, 1931 – June 16, 2023

Photo by Christopher Michel

A fearless and inspiring truth teller,
Daniel Ellsberg advocated for peace,
freedom of information,
and civil courage.

Contents

Foreword

ALAN MACLEOD

We are swimming in an ocean of propaganda—not that we usually call it that. We like to think of propaganda as something that exists largely in "enemy" nations, such as China or North Korea. But what else to call the thousands of misleading advertisements, news snippets, or politicized messages we see every day?[1] Given the prevalence of PR, spin, and bias out there, added to the fact that US schools seldom teach media literacy adequately, it is little wonder that many Americans are drowning in propaganda—even if they don't recognize it as such.

Trust in journalism is at an all-time low. A 2022 Gallup poll found that just one-in-nine Americans had confidence in TV news, and fewer than one-in-six believed in the printed press.[2] A subsequent survey released in February 2023 revealed that half of Americans believe national news organizations intentionally deceive the public in order to suit their own agendas.[3]

As a former media studies academic who is now a journalist, all I can say is they are right to be skeptical. The industry is every bit as deceitful, nefarious, and corrupt as most Americans suspect. Establishment media, in short, is not our friend. For the most part, media are gigantic for-profit corporate structures with their own interests—interests that are often antithetical to those of the public.

With some notable exceptions, corporate news outlets have largely abandoned their professed role as the fourth estate. In other words, corporate media do not challenge power; they are power, the voice of the powerful. And power deserves to be scrutinized.

Today, a handful of huge corporations controls the vast majority of what Americans see, read, or hear daily. Unlike much of the world, the United States does not have a large state media empire. We are taught to see state media as inherently untrustworthy, something enemy states use to propagandize their populations. But if corporations have captured our government, isn't corporate media state media by default? After all, the same people and organizations that fund our politicians also own and bankroll our press.

This collapse in media trust is part of a generalized decline of faith in institutions. Even if members of the public do not express it as succinctly as the philosopher and public intellectual John Ralston Saul, who described the country as going through a "corporate coup d'état in slow motion," people see how their nation is being hollowed out for profit, as jobs are sent abroad and corporations are allowed to pillage the state.

America rarely hears it framed like this on the news, however. Nearly half the independent news stories highlighted in Chapter 1 of *State of the Free Press 2024* demonstrate how corporate news media have ignored crucial news stories of this sort.

Unfortunately, while distrust is high, Americans often see media bias through a highly partisan lens. Audiences are hyper-polarized: 93 percent of Fox News viewers are or lean Republican, while 91 percent of *New York Times* readers and 95 percent of MSNBC's audience skew Democrat.[4] This leads to a shallow understanding and scrutiny of the corporate press; *our* media is honest, *theirs* is propaganda and fake news.

This superficial, partisan framework of understanding was on show when billionaire plutocrat Elon Musk purchased Twitter in October 2022. Liberals were aghast, while conservatives cheered him on as a supposed warrior for free speech. Few seemed interested in what the implications of the (then) world's richest man taking over one of the planet's chief arteries of communications would be, beyond whether it was good for Team Red or Team Blue.

Putting our faith in one or another oligarch to save us is a recipe for disaster. For the most part, the internet and social media suffer from the same problems as legacy media. Only a handful of monopolistic profit-seeking mega-corporations dominate online. These companies are also intimately connected to the US national security state, which has leaned on them to suppress speech and content that challenges their interests, as I explored in the #2 story featured in Chapter 1 of this volume. With a quiet tweak of their algorithms, companies such as Google, Twitter, and Facebook wield the power to boost or throttle media content. In the wake of the 2016 election and ensuing moral panic around fake news, big social media companies reoriented their algorithms to promote what they called "authoritative" reporting content and suppress "borderline" content.

The effect was to invisibly suffocate high-quality independent media outlets and channel people back to corporate legacy media, in effect, turning the internet back into a place safe for advertisers who call the shots.

Overnight, *Democracy Now!* lost 36 percent of its Google traffic, The Intercept, 19 percent.[5] MintPress News, where I work, saw its Google traffic fall by around 90 percent.

The solution to navigating this confusing media landscape is developing what philosopher and media critic Noam Chomsky long ago called a course of "intellectual self-defense."[6] And the answer to the problem of an unrepresentative media is to build new structures, outlets and organizations that can provide an alternative and an antidote to the establishment.

On both of these issues, Project Censored is leading the way. For decades, their excellent research and output has helped develop a critical media literacy among their readers, providing a crucial framework to aid people in scrutinizing what they are consuming. Just as Socrates said "an unexamined life is not worth living" so an unexamined article is not worth reading.

Year-on-year, Project Censored's meticulously compiled list of the top "Censored" news stories has become essential reading for media critics, scholars, and forward-thinking individuals wishing to inform themselves about the biggest issues corporate media are not talking about. Meanwhile, their weekly radio show keeps listeners up to date on crucial questions and debates the corporate press ignore in favor of serving up junk food news. It is, therefore, an honor to be asked to pen this foreword.

As you will find out, sometimes, stories are too important to cover—meaning that their ramifications would be too wide-reaching or their consequences too damaging to the powerful interests that hold sway over most all of our means of communication. In these cases, they are either back-paged, downplayed, or simply ignored. Thankfully, Project Censored is on the case, showing the way where corporate media fear to tread.

ALAN MACLEOD, PHD, is Senior Staff Writer and Podcast Producer for MintPress News. The editor of *Propaganda in the Information Age: Still Manufacturing Consent* and author of *Bad News From Venezuela: Twenty Years of Fake News and Misreporting*, he has also contributed to a number of media outlets, including FAIR, the *Guardian*, the New Statesman, Salon, *Jacobin*, and Common Dreams.

Notes

1   For one example of what this looks like, see Jon Simpson, "Finding Brand Success in the Digital World," *Forbes*, August 25, 2017.
2   Jeffrey M. Jones, "Confidence in U.S. Institutions Down; Average at New Low," Gallup, July 5, 2022.
3   "American Views 2022: Part 2, Trust Media and Democracy," Knight Foundation, February 15, 2023.
4   Elizabeth Grieco, "Americans' Main Sources for Political News Vary by Party and Age," Pew Research Center, April 1, 2020.
5   Andre Damon and David North, "Google's New Search Protocol Is Restricting Access to 13 Leading Socialist, Progressive and Anti-war Web Sites," World Socialist Web Site, August 2, 2017.
6   Noam Chomsky, "False, False, False, and False," *Talk of the Nation* (NPR), interview by Ray Saurez, January 20, 1999.

What If Journalism Disappeared?[1]

ANDY LEE ROTH and MICKEY HUFF

In 1995, early in the development of the global internet, sociologist Michael Schudson imagined how people might process information if journalism were to suddenly disappear. An expert on the history of US news media, Schudson speculated that peoples' need to identify the day's most important and relevant news from the continuous torrent of available information would eventually lead to the reinvention of journalism.[2]

Beyond daily gossip, practical advice, or mere information, Schudson contended, people desire what he called "public knowledge," or news, the demand for which made it difficult to imagine a world without journalism.

Nearly thirty years later, many Americans live in a version of the world remarkably close to the one Schudson pondered in 1995—because either they lack access to news or they choose to ignore journalism in favor of other, more sensational content.

By exploring how journalism is increasingly absent from many Americans' lives, we can identify false paths and promising routes to its reinvention.

THE RISE OF NEWS DESERTS

Many communities across the United States now suffer from limited access to credible, comprehensive local news. Northwestern University's 2022 "State of Local News" report determined that more than half of the counties in the United States—some 1,630—are served by only one newspaper each, while another two hundred or more counties, the homes of some four million people, have no newspaper at all.[3] Put another way, seventy million Americans—a fifth of the country's population—live in "news deserts," communities with very limited access to local news, or in counties just one newspaper closure away from becoming so.

Not surprisingly, the study found that news deserts are most common in economically struggling communities, which also frequently lack affordable and reliable high-speed digital service—a form of inequality known as digital redlining.[4] Members of such communities are doubly impacted: lacking local news sources, they are also cut off from online access to the country's surviving regional and national newspapers.

Noting that credible news "feeds grassroots democracy and builds a sense of belonging to a community," Penny Abernathy, the report's author, wrote that news deserts contribute to "the malignant spread of misinformation and disinformation, political polarization, eroding trust in media, and a yawning digital and economic divide among citizens."

DIVIDED ATTENTION AND "NEWS SNACKING"

While the rise of news deserts makes credible news a scarce resource for many Americans, others show no more than passing interest in news. A February 2022 Gallup/ Knight Foundation poll found that only 33 percent of Americans reported paying "a great deal" of attention to national news, with even lower figures for local news (21 percent) and international news (12 percent).[5]

With the increasing prevalence of smartphone ownership and reliance on social media, news outlets now face ferocious competition for peoples' attention.[6] Following news is an incidental activity in the lives of many who engage in "news snacking." As communications scholar Hektor Haarkötter described in a 2022 article, "Discarded News," mobile internet use has altered patterns of news consumption: "News is no longer received consciously, but rather consumed incidentally like potato chips."[7] Instead of intentionally seeking news from sources dedicated to journalism, many people now assume the viral nature of social media will automatically alert them to any truly important events or issues, a belief that is especially prominent among younger media users, Haarkötter noted. A 2017 study determined that the prevalence of this "news-finds-me" perception is likely "to widen gaps in political knowledge" while promoting "a false sense of being informed."[8]

SIGNS OF REINVENTION?

With journalism inaccessible to the growing number of people who live in "news deserts," or only a matter of passing interest to online "news snackers," the disappearance of journalism that Schudson pondered hypothetically in 1995 is a reality for many people today. If journalism as we have known it is on the verge of disappearing, are there also—as Schudson predicted—signs of its reinvention?

Examining the profession itself, the signs are not all that encouraging.

Consider, for example, the pivot by many independent journalists to Substack, Patreon, and other digital platforms in order to reach their audiences directly. Reader-supported journalism may be a necessary survival reflex, but we are wary of pinning the future of journalism on tech platforms controlled by third parties not necessarily committed to principles of ethical journalism, as advocated by the Society of Professional Journalists.[9]

Media companies—including the tech website CNET and BuzzFeed—have experimented with using artificial intelligence programs, including the infamous ChatGPT bot, to produce content.[10] Noting that there would be "nothing surprising" about AI technology eventually threatening jobs in journalism, Hamilton Nolan of *In These Times* suggested that journalists have two key resources in the "looming fight" with AI, unions and "a widely accepted code of ethics that dictates how far standards can be pushed before something no longer counts as journalism."[11] News outlets, Nolan argued, do not simply publish stories, they can also explain, when necessary, *how* a story was produced. The credibility of journalists and news outlets hinges on that accountability. Artificial intelligence may be able to produce media "content"—it may even be of use to journalists in news gathering—but it cannot produce journalism.

We also don't anticipate a revival of journalism on the basis of the June 2022 memo from CNN's Chris Licht, shortly after he became the network's CEO, which directed staff to avoid overuse of its "breaking news" banner. "We are truth-tellers, focused on informing, not alarming our viewers," Licht wrote in his memo.[12] But competitive pressures will continue to drive commercial news outlets to lure their audiences' inconstant attention with sensational reporting and clickbait headlines.

TOWARD A PUBLIC OPTION

More promising bases for the reinvention of journalism will depend not on technological fixes or more profitable business models but on reinvesting in journalism as a public good.

In a 2020 article for *Jacobin*, media scholar Victor Pickard argued that commercial media "can't support the bare minimum levels of news media . . . that democracy requires."[13] Drawing on the late sociologist Erik Olin Wright's model for constructing alternatives to capitalism, Pickard argued that the creation of a publicly-owned media system is the most direct way "to tame and erode commercial media."[14]

The "public options" championed by Pickard and others—which include significant budgets to support nonprofit media institutions and municipal broadband networks—would do much to address the conditions that have exiled far too many Americans to news deserts.

If the public option advocated by Pickard focuses on the production of better quality news, the reinvention of journalism will also depend on cultivating broader public interest in and support for top-notch journalism. Here, perhaps ironically, some of the human desires that social media have so effectively harnessed might be redirected in support of investigative journalism that exposes abuses of power and addresses social inequalities.

REMEMBERING A GOLDEN ERA OF MUCKRAKING

Few living Americans recall Ida Mae Tarbell, Lincoln Steffens, Upton Sinclair, and other pioneering investigative journalists who worked in the aftermath of the Gilded Age—an era, comparable to ours, when a thin veneer of extravagant economic prosperity for a narrow elite helped camouflage underlying social disintegration. "Muckraker" journalists exposed political and economic corruption in ways that captivated the public's attention and spurred societal reform.

For instance, in a series of investigative reports published by *McClure's Magazine* between October 1902 and November 1903, Steffens exposed local stories of collusion between corrupt politicians and businessmen in St. Louis, Minneapolis, Pittsburgh, Philadelphia, and New York. Most significantly, though, Steffens's "Shame of the Cities" series, published as a book in 1904, drew significant public attention to a *national* pattern of civic decay.[15]

Steffens's reporting not only made him a household name, it also spurred rival publications to pursue their own muckraking investigations. As his biographer, Peter Hartshorn, wrote, other publishers "quickly grasped what the public was demanding: articles that not only entertained and informed but also exposed. Americans were captivated by the muckrakers and their ability to provide names, dollar amounts, and other titillating specifics."[16]

By alerting the public to systemic abuses of power, investigative journalism galvanized popular support for political reform, and indirectly helped propel a wave of progressive legislation. As Carl Jensen related in *Stories That Changed America*, the muckrakers' investigative reporting led to "a nation-wide public revolt against social evils" and "a decade of reforms in antitrust legislation, the electoral process, banking regulations, and a host of other social programs."[17] The golden age of muckraking came to an end when the United States entered World War I, diverting national attention from domestic issues to conflict overseas.

Though largely forgotten, the muckraking journalists from the last century provide another model of how journalism might be renewed, if not reinvented. The muckrakers' reporting was successful in part because it harnessed a public appetite for shame and scandal to the cause of political engagement. To paraphrase one of Schudson's points about news as public knowledge, the muckrakers' reporting served as a crucial resource for "people ready to take political action." An appreciation of the links between trustworthy information, relevant news, and political action informs the contents of Project Censored's *State of the Free Press 2024*.

INSIDE *STATE OF THE FREE PRESS 2024*

Chapter 1 presents Project Censored's twenty-five most important but under-reported news stories of 2022-2023. This chapter highlights the crucial roles played by independent journalists and news outlets in bringing to light important issues that their corporate counterparts have either marginalized or omitted. The news topics they cover have otherwise been "censored" in the broad sense established by Project Censored founder Carl Jensen, who defined censorship as "the suppression of information, whether purposeful or not, by any method—including bias, omission, underreporting or self-censorship—that prevents the public from fully knowing what is happening in its society."[18] From activism to reform outdated laws that criminalize HIV (story #25), to the economic costs of gun violence (#19), and the discovery of toxic "forever chemicals" in rainwater (this year's #1 story), the stories presented in this chapter address social issues on which the public might be motivated to act, were it better informed by corporate news media. Compiled and edited by Libby Meagher, Grace Harty, Amy Grim Buxbaum, Steve Macek, and Andy Lee Roth, this year's Top 25 story list represents the collective effort of 220 students from twelve colleges and university campuses who identified, vetted, and summarized Validated Independent News stories through the Project's Campus Affiliates Program.

In Chapter 2, Grace Harty, Kathleen Minelli, Nicole Mendez-Villarrubia, and Steve Macek revisit four Top 25 stories from previous Project Censored yearbooks to update subsequent developments in those stories and to reassess the extent to which they remain blockaded by corporate news outlets. This year's Déjà Vu News chapter reviews reporting on the crisis of missing and murdered Indigenous women and girls, first covered as the #1 story in *State of the Free Press 2021*; the shadow network of conservative outlets that emerged from the collapse of local news outlets, reported as story #6 in the 2021 yearbook; US women facing prison sentences for miscarriages, story #8 in *Censored 2020*; and corporate news media understating the prevalence of rape and sexual violence, previously reported in story #22 from *Censored 2015*.

This year's Junk Food News makes a buffet for Chapter 3 as Jen Lyons, Sierra Kaul, Reagan Haynie, Marcelle Levine

Swinburne, Gavin Kelley, and Mickey Huff serve up recycled refuse of news no one can use. From the Faux-lanthropy of YouTube sensation MrBeast, spy balloons, and UFOs to March Murder Madness in basketball, and a smorgasbord of sensational distractions, this year's chapter presents a full menu of Junk Food News. Instead of all this junk, the corporate media could have been reporting about: how our for-profit healthcare system is truly ill, the environmental fallout from a train derailment in Ohio that will linger for years, an injustice system that routinely privileges the wealthy, and how the state of Utah is eviscerating civil liberties for environmental activists.

In Chapter 4, Robin Andersen examines News Abuse, the term Project Censored uses to describe genuinely newsworthy topics that the public is, nevertheless, unlikely to grasp fully due to slanted corporate news coverage. This year Andersen highlights news abuse in corporate reporting on embattled Republican congressman and serial fabulist George Santos, the February 2023 Ohio train derailment disaster, the ongoing Russian invasion of Ukraine, and the September 2022 Nord Stream pipeline sabotage. Andersen critiques the corporate media's reliance on "standardized framing, jingoistic rhetoric, and distractions or outright fabrications" that misinform the public by shielding elite individuals, powerful corporations, and the US empire from due scrutiny.

Chapter 5, Media Democracy in Action, features individuals and organizations dedicated to countering extremism, polarization, and misinformation by championing truth telling, peace building, human rights, and ethically-committed journalism. Edited and introduced by Mischa Geracoulis, this year's chapter includes contributions from Maria Armoudian and Olivia Guyodo, who examine how the governments of Turkey and Azerbaijan suppress accurate reporting and promote propaganda about ethnic Armenians and the Artsakh independence movement; Christine Emeran, director of the Youth Free Expression Program at the National Coalition Against Censorship, on organized, politically-driven efforts to ban books in US schools; Jen Senko, creator of the documentary film *The Brainwashing of My Dad*, on the "Fox News model" of propaganda; and Rebecca Vincent of Reporters Without Borders, on protecting journalism in an era defined by national security. As Geracoulis writes in the chapter's introduction, each of these women is working to "uphold the guardrails of free and independent media" in ways that should inspire readers to join them in protecting and promoting media democracy.

In Chapter 6, Maximillian Alvarez, editor-in-chief at the *Real News Network*, reflects on the democratic function of a free press and what it means to do journalism. For Alvarez, this means focusing attention on topics and experiences that are often devalued or erased by corporate media—including the stories of working people, the connection between the workplace and democracy, and the uplifting truths that "we deserve to live with dignity, that we have rights, that things don't have to be this way, that they could be better, and that we have it within our power to make it so." Based on his keynote address at the 2022 Critical Media Literacy Conference of the Americas, Alvarez's call to action provides a resoundingly positive conclusion to *State of the Free Press 2024*.

REVIVING PUBLIC HUNGER FOR NEWS ABOUT "WHAT'S REALLY GOING ON"

Despite its imperiled status, journalism that serves the public good has not yet disappeared.

As the diverse contributors to this book make clear, there is no shortage of exemplary independent reporting on the injustices and inequalities that threaten to disintegrate today's United States.

That said, it is not simple to recognize such reporting or to find sources of it, amidst the clattering voices that compete for the public's attention. Finding authentic news requires not only countering the spread of news deserts, but also cultivating the public's taste for news that goes deeper than the latest TikTok trend, celebrity gossip, or talking head "hot takes."

A public option for journalism could help assure more widespread access to vital news and diverse perspectives; and a revival of the muckraking tradition, premised on journalism that informs the public by exposing abuses of authority, could reconnect people who have otherwise lost interest in news that distracts, sensationalizes, or—perhaps worse—polarizes us.

Both the twentieth-century muckrakers and today's advocates of journalism in the public interest provide lessons about how journalism can help recreate a shared sense of community—a value touted in Northwestern's 2022 "State of Local News" report. The muckrakers appealed to a collective sense of outrage that wealthy tycoons and crooked politicians might deceive and fleece the public. That outrage brought people together to respond in common cause.

As George Seldes—a torchbearer of the muckraking tradition, who founded *In Fact*, the nation's first successful periodical of press criticism, in 1940—often noted, journalism is about telling people "what's really going on" in society.[19] At its most influential, journalism promotes public awareness that spurs civic engagement, real reform, and even radical change.

Perhaps that is why it is so difficult, especially in these troubled times, to imagine a world without journalism. Our best hopes for the future, including the renewal of community and grassroots democracy, all hinge at least partly on what Schudson called "public knowledge," which a robust free press protects and promotes.

Andy Lee Roth, Winthrop, Washington
Mickey Huff, Fair Oaks, California
June 2023

Notes

1   This introduction updates and expands an article originally published as Andy Lee Roth and Mickey Huff, "What If Journalism Disappeared?" Dispatches from Project Censored, October 20, 2022.

2   Michael Schudson, "Introduction: News as Public Knowledge," in *The Power of News* (Cambridge, MA: Harvard University Press, 1995), 2.

3   Penny Abernathy, "The State of Local News: The 2022 Report," Local News Initiative (Northwestern University), June 29, 2022.

4   For the Project's previous coverage of the history of redlining and its digital legacy, see Payton Blair et al., "Poor Infrastructure, a Legacy of Discriminatory Redlining, Inhibits Rural Black Americans' Internet Access," story #19 in *State of the Free Press 2023*, eds. Mickey Huff and Andy Lee Roth (Fair Oaks, CA and New York: The Censored Press and Seven Stories Press), 87-9, and available online via the Project Censored website.

5   Sarah Fioroni and RJ Reinhart, "Americans' Attention to National News Lowest in Four Years," Knight Foundation, February 17, 2022.

6   Federica Laricchia, "Smartphone Ownership in the U.S. 2011-2021," Statista, December 6, 2022; "Social Media Fact Sheet," Pew Research Center, April 7, 2021 (updated January 11, 2022).

7   Hektor Haarkötter, "Discarded News: On News Enlightenment, Agenda Cutting, and News Ignorance," *Journalism Research* 5, no. 2 (February 2022): 114-33, quotation at 124.

8   Homero Gil de Zúñiga, Brian Weeks, and Alberto Ardèvol-Abreu, "Effects of the News-Finds-Me Perception in Communication: Social Media Use Implications for News Seeking and Learning About Politics," *Journal of Computer-Mediated Communication* 22, no. 3 (May 1, 2017): 105–123, quotations at 108, 119.

9   "SPJ Code of Ethics," Society of Professional Journalists, September 6, 2014.

10   See, for example, Mia Sato, "CNET Pauses Publishing AI-Written Stories After Disclosure Controversy,"The Verge, January 20, 2023; Oliver Darcy, "Buzzfeed Says It Will Use AI to Help Create Content, Stock Jumps 150%," CNN Business, January 26, 2023.

11   Hamilton Nolan, "How to Stop AI From Eating Journalism," *In These Times*, February 8, 2023.

12   Brian Steinberg, "CNN's New Chief Says 'Breaking News' Banner Is Overused," *Variety*, June 2, 2022. In June 2023, CNN reported that the network's chairman and CEO was "out after a brief and tumultuous tenure." See Oliver Darcy, "CNN Chairman and CEO Chris Licht Is Out After a Brief and Tumultuous Tenure," CNN, June 7, 2023.

13   Victor Pickard, "We Need a Media System That Serves People's Needs, Not Corporations',"*Jacobin*, January 27, 2020. See also Veronica Vasquez and Mickey Huff, "Revive Journalism With a Stimulus Package and Public Option," story #10 in Project Censored's *State of the Free Press 2021*, eds. Mickey Huff and Andy Lee Roth (New York: Seven Stories Press), 62-65, also available online at the Project Censored website; and Mark Lloyd, "Don't Laugh, There Is a Policy Solution to the Problem of American Journalism," ScheerPost, May 3, 2023.

14   Erik Olin Wright, "How to Be an Anticapitalist Today," *Jacobin*, December 2, 2015.

15   Lincoln Steffens, *The Shame of the Cities* (New York: McClure, Phillips & Co., 1904), available online via Project Gutenberg.

16   Peter Hartshorn, *I Have Seen the Future: A Life of Lincoln Steffens* (Berkeley, CA: Counterpoint Press, 2012), 103.

17   Carl Jensen, *Stories That Changed America: Muckrakers of the 20th Century* (New York: Seven Stories Press, 2002), 18.

18   Carl Jensen, "Project Censored: Raking Muck, Raising Hell," in *Censored: The News That Didn't Make the News—and Why*, ed. Carl Jensen (Chapel Hill, North Carolina: Shelburne Press, 1993), 1–14, 7.

19   George Seldes' pioneering journal, *In Fact*, remains available through the Internet Archive. See, for example, *In Fact* 1, no. 1 (May 20, 1940).

CHAPTER 1

The Top *Censored* Stories and Media Analysis of 2022–2023

Compiled and edited by
LIBBY MEAGHER, GRACE HARTY, AMY GRIM BUXBAUM,
STEVE MACEK, and ANDY LEE ROTH

INTRODUCTION: LIGHT THROUGH THE SLATS

ANDY LEE ROTH AND STEVE MACEK

The power of news is often described using visual metaphors. Good journalism is said to be illuminating, meaning it provides clarity and insight; exemplary reporting is praised for "shining light" on a subject or "bringing to light" crucial facts and original perspectives. One major US newspaper, the *Washington Post*, uses the slogan "Democracy Dies in Darkness" to promote its brand and, presumably, the value of journalism more generally; and the concept of "framing," a fundamental element of critical media literacy, portrays news as a "window" to the world, yet another visual metaphor.[1]

Extending these metaphors of vision and illumination, the news reports featured in this chapter are rays of light shining through a heavily slatted window. Each of these independent news reports highlights a social issue that has otherwise been dimly lit or altogether obscured by corporate news outlets. The shading slats are built from the corporate media's concentrated ownership, reliance on advertising, relationship to political power, and narrow definitions of who and what count as "newsworthy." Censorship, whether overt or subtle, establishes the angle of the slats, admitting more or less light from outside. Put another way, independent reporting on these topics—light shining through the slats—represents the influence of independent journalism to challenge the corporate news media's hegemonic worldview.

One fundamental purpose of Project Censored's annual Top 25 story list is to draw greater attention to important issues that we only know about because of intrepid reporting by independent journalists and news organizations. From activism to reform outdated laws that criminalize HIV (see story #25) to the economic costs of gun violence (#19) and the discovery of toxic "forever chemicals" in rainwater (this year's #1 story), each of the stories presented in this chapter is important in its own right and represents an issue on which the public might be motivated to act, were it better informed.

But it is also important to grasp the Project's 2022-23 story list as the latest installment in an ongoing effort to identify systemic gaps in so-called "mainstream" (i.e., corporate) news coverage. Examining public issues that independent journalists and outlets have reported but which fall outside the scope of corporate news coverage makes it possible to document *in specific detail* how corporate news media leave the public in the dark by marginalizing or blockading crucial issues, limiting political debate, and promoting corporate views and interests. To Project Censored's existing database of 1,175 news topics and stories neglected by the establishment press, *State of the Free Press 2024* adds twenty-five new data points.

Examining connections between stories within this

year's Top 25 list can be a first step in recognizing patterns of omission or marginalization in corporate framing of what is newsworthy. One of the most obvious of these omissions is the corporate news media's apparent reluctance to cover the grinding consequences of immense, systemic economic inequalities, as highlighted by independent press reporting on record-high corporate profits (story #10), a looming debt crisis for the world's poorest nations (#18), and the reality that nearly half of all unhoused people in the United States are employed (#21).

Another major theme of independent journalism evident in this year's story list is the corrosive influence of the fossil fuel industry. In efforts to maintain their economic interests and political influence, fossil fuel investors are suing national governments to thwart climate regulations (story #7) and using donations to universities to skew climate and energy research (#12), even as climate change has forced entire tribal towns to relocate (#11), and new research further documents the threats of oil and gas extraction to human health, including especially mothers and young children (#8). Thanks to the work of independent journalists, we also know that rainforest carbon offset programs—as endorsed by Shell, Disney, and other internationally renowned corporations—are often "worthless" (story #5) and that the fossil fuel industry was not alone in hiding its knowledge of the climate crisis from the public: Electric utility companies have also been knowingly spreading misinformation about climate change for decades (#14).

The 2024 story list also includes a cluster of stories that illuminate the nuanced realities of censorship in the twenty-first century. Big Tech companies, including Google,

Meta, and Microsoft, are hiring former employees of US and Israeli intelligence agencies for senior positions, affording them significant influence over online communication, commerce, and information gathering (story #2); US government agencies have pressured Twitter to constrain political content on the popular social networking service (#24); and leaked Department of Homeland Security documents revealed new details of its efforts to ramp up censorship of online speech through the development of a "Disinformation Governance Board" (#17). Five additional news stories—noted below as Honorable Mentions—provide further evidence of digital-age censorship, including independent coverage of a Biden administration "gag order" on federal scientists and the use of bogus copyright complaints to throttle investigative journalism.

In 1920, Walter Lippmann, a leading media critic of his era, issued a clarion call: "The news about the news needs to be told," Lippmann wrote.[2] Since 1976, college students working with Project Censored have done just that. Each of the stories originally covered by independent journalists and news organizations has been reviewed and vetted by students and their faculty mentors participating in Project Censored's Campus Affiliates Program. (College teachers and students: We invite you to join us in this work. Learn more about opportunities under the "Classroom" tab on the Project Censored website.) The multiple stages of the year-long review process are described in detail in the "Note on Research and Evaluation of *Censored* News Stories" below.

This year's Top 25 chapter represents the collective effort of 220 students from twelve college and university campuses across the United States who have developed and engaged their critical media literacy skills by identifying, vetting, and summarizing important but under-reported independent news stories. They are the forty-eighth cohort of students who have worked with Project Censored to expose and publicize what its founder, Carl Jensen, called "The News That Didn't Make the News—and Why."

We hope this year's *Censored* story list will be illuminating. Perhaps one or more of these stories will even motivate you to join the independent journalists, student researchers, and Project Censored in speaking out about these important but often overshadowed issues. Focusing attention on what Lippmann called "the news about the news" helps to reveal the operation of otherwise taken-for-granted "slats" that filter our news and privilege elite interests, permitting the light of independent journalism that serves the public good to shine more brightly.

ACKNOWLEDGMENTS: Thanks to Gavin Kelley, Riley Cummins, and Ashton Sidford for research assistance during the final vetting of this year's top *Censored* stories. We are also grateful to Zach McNanna for research and writing of additional Validated Independent News stories.

NOTE ON RESEARCH AND EVALUATION OF
CENSORED NEWS STORIES

How do we at Project Censored identify and evaluate independent news stories, and how do we know that the Top 25 stories that we bring forward each year are not only relevant and significant but also trustworthy? The answer is that every candidate news story undergoes rigorous review, which takes place in multiple stages during each annual cycle. Although adapted to take advantage of both the Project's expanding affiliates program and current technologies, the vetting process is quite similar to the one Project Censored founder Carl Jensen established more than forty years ago.

Candidate stories are initially identified by Project Censored professors and students or are nominated by members of the general public, who bring them to the Project's attention.[3] Together, faculty and students evaluate each candidate story in terms of its importance, timeliness, quality of sources, and inadequate corporate news coverage. If it fails on any one of these criteria, the story is deemed inappropriate and is excluded from further consideration.

Once Project Censored receives the candidate story, we undertake a second round of judgment, using the same criteria and updating the review to include any subsequent, competing corporate coverage. We post stories that pass this round of review on the Project's website as Validated Independent News stories (VINs).[4]

In early spring, we present all VINs in the current cycle to the faculty and students at all of our affiliate campuses, and to our panel of expert judges, who cast votes to winnow the candidate stories from more than one hundred to twenty-five.

Once the Top 25 list has been determined, Project Censored student interns begin another intensive review of each story using Nexis Uni and ProQuest databases. Additional faculty and students contribute to this final stage of review.

The Top 25 finalists are then sent to our panel of judges, whose votes rank them in numerical order. At the same time, these experts—including media studies professors, professional journalists and editors, and a former commissioner of the Federal Communications Commission—offer their insights on the stories' strengths and weaknesses.[5]

Thus, by the time a story appears on the pages of the *State of the Free Press* yearbook, it has undergone at least five distinct rounds of review and evaluation.

Although the stories that Project Censored brings forward may be socially and politically controversial—and sometimes even psychologically challenging—we are confident that each is the result of serious journalistic effort and deserves greater public attention.

THE TOP *CENSORED* STORIES AND MEDIA ANALYSIS OF 2022-2023

"Forever Chemicals" in Rainwater a Global Threat to Human Health

Morgan McFall-Johnsen, "Rainwater Is No Longer Safe to Drink Anywhere on Earth Due to 'Forever Chemicals' Linked to Cancer, Study Suggests," *Insider*, August 13, 2022.

Student Researcher: Grace Harty (North Central College)

Faculty Evaluator: Steve Macek (North Central College)

Environmental scientists have found hazardous levels of manufactured chemicals in rainwater, leading to the dramatic conclusion that rainwater is "no longer safe to drink anywhere on Earth," according to an August 2022 report from Insider. Morgan McFall-Johnsen's article reported results from a global study of per- and polyfluoroalkyl substances (PFAS) conducted by researchers from Stockholm University and the Institute of Biogeochemistry and Pollutant Dynamics at ETH Zurich. In an August 2022 report published in the journal *Environmental Science & Technology*, scientists concluded that "in many areas inhabited by humans," PFAS contamination levels in rainwater, surface water, and soil "often greatly exceed" the strictest international guidelines for acceptable levels of perfluoroalkyl acids.[6]

To reach this conclusion, the researchers compared levels of perfluorooctanoic acid (PFOA) and perfluorooctanesulfonic acid (PFOS) in rainwater from around the world with the drinking water guidelines established by environmental agencies in the United States and Denmark, "which are the most stringent advisories known globally," the researchers reported. Based on the latest US guidelines for PFOA in drinking water, "rainwater everywhere would be judged unsafe to drink," the lead author of the study, Ian Cousins, stated in a post on the Stockholm University website.[7] Cousins drew even more dire conclusions in an August 2022 interview: "We have crossed a planetary boundary," the researcher told Agence France-Presse, "We have made the planet inhospitable to human life . . . [N]othing is clean anymore."[8]

The PFAS the researchers examined are known informally as "forever chemicals" because they take a long time to break down, "allowing them to build up in people, animals, and environments," Insider reported. Prior research has linked these chemicals to prostate, kidney, and testicular cancer and additional health risks, including developmental delays in children, decreased fertility in women and men, reduced vaccine efficacy, and high cholesterol.[9]

In June 2022, the US Environmental Protection Agency (EPA) issued interim updated drinking water health advisories for PFOA and PFOS. According to the agency, the updated advisory levels were "based on new science," including findings that "some negative health effects may occur with concentrations of PFOA or PFOS in water that are near zero."[10] As Insider reported, the EPA had previously set seventy parts per trillion as acceptable levels for PFOA and PFOS in drinking water. In its June 2022 advisory, the EPA set interim guidelines to 0.004 parts per trillion for PFOA and 0.02 parts per trillion for PFOS.

The news that rainwater is no longer safe to drink due to PFAS contamination has received limited corporate news coverage. In an August 2022 article about the EPA's decision to label two "forever chemicals" as hazardous, the *Washington Post* mentioned that "even some rainwater is tainted with PFAS at dangerously high levels, according to one recent study."[11] In April 2022, before the publication of the Stockholm University/ETH Zurich study, a *New York Times* report on the prevalence of PFAS made passing reference to how these substances have "found their way into rainwater, soil, sediment, ice caps, and outdoor and indoor plants."[12] Beyond the most prestigious US newspapers, the study's findings have received more detailed coverage from *USA Today*, the Discovery Channel, and Medical News Today.[13]

Corporate outlets have done more to cover a developing series of lawsuits against chemical manufacturing companies that use PFAS in their products. In December 2022, the *Wall Street Journal* reported that, in response to growing "criticism and litigation" over alleged health and environmental impacts, the multinational conglomerate 3M will "stop making forever chemicals and cease using them by the end of 2025."[14] As this volume goes to press, several states—including California, Maine, New Mexico, Maryland, and Rhode Island—have brought or are bringing litigation against 3M and other companies for significant harm to residents and natural resources caused by "forever chemicals." CNBC reported that the PFAS trial "could set the tone for future lawsuits."[15] In June 2023, three US-based chemical companies—DuPont, and two spin-off companies, Chemours and Corteva—reached a $1.18 billion deal to resolve complaints of polluting drinking water systems with potentially harmful "forever chemicals."[16] The same month, researchers at the University of California, San Francisco, published a study in the *Annals of Global Health* using internal industry documents to show that the companies responsible for "forever chemicals" have known for decades that these substances pose significant threats to human health and the environment.[17]

See "Toxic Chemicals Continue to Go Unregulated in United States," story #3 in this chapter, for related coverage.

Hiring of Former CIA Employees and Ex-Israeli Agents "Blurs Line" Between Big Tech and Big Brother

Alan MacLeod, "National Security Search Engine: Google's Ranks Are Filled With CIA Agents," MintPress News, July 25, 2022.

Alan MacLeod, "Revealed: The Former Israeli Spies Working In Top Jobs at Google, Facebook and Microsoft," MintPress News, October 31, 2022.

Student Researcher: Reagan Haynie (Loyola Marymount University)

Faculty Advisor: Mickey Huff (Diablo Valley College)

Former employees of US and Israeli intelligence agencies now hold senior positions at Google, Meta, Microsoft, and other tech giants, where these individuals influence policy and control programs that regulate internet users' access to information, Alan MacLeod reported in a pair of stories published by MintPress News in July and October 2022.

Google has hired former Central Intelligence Agency (CIA) employees to fill sensitive positions, affording them significant influence over the operation of the world's most used search engine and other Google products that encompass online communication, commerce, and information gathering. As MacLeod reported in July 2022, based on his analysis of employment websites and databases, a former CIA employee is working in almost every department at Google.

Google's recruitment of former CIA officers is cause for alarm because of the agency's history of misinformation and disinformation "to further the goals of the national security state," MacLeod wrote. In a 1983 interview, former CIA intelligence officer John Stockwell, author of *In Search of Enemies*, described the dissemination of propaganda as a "major function" of the agency.[18] Stockwell described how the CIA worked to place false news stories in foreign newspapers, which global news agencies such as Reuters and AFP subsequently used, unwittingly, as sources for reports of their own. "It was pure, raw, false propaganda," Stockwell said in an interview quoted in MacLeod's report.

As Google hires more former CIA officers, one risk is that it "will start to think like and see problems the same way as the CIA does," MacLeod warned. Elizabeth

Murray, a retired intelligence agent who worked as a CIA analyst, noted that the close relationship between the CIA and Google "threatens individual rights to privacy, free speech, freedom of expression." Ultimately, MacLeod concluded, "the line between big tech and big brother has been blurred beyond recognition."

In October 2022, MacLeod reported that "hundreds of former agents" of Unit 8200, an Israeli intelligence organization, comparable to the United States National Security Agency (NSA), hold influential positions at the world's biggest tech companies, including Google, Microsoft, Facebook, and Amazon. As MacLeod reported, Unit 8200 is "infamous for surveilling the indigenous Palestinian population," was implicated in the Pegasus spyware scandal that made headlines in 2021, and "likely aided" in the 2018 killing of Saudi journalist Jamal Khashoggi.

Using the professional networking website LinkedIn, MacLeod identified more than ninety-nine former Unit 8200 agents currently working at Google. The number is probably much higher since it only accounts for employees with public LinkedIn profiles that list a connection to the unit. The Israeli Defense Force (IDF) instructs veterans to keep their association with the unit private, which makes the total number of Unit 8200 affiliated employees difficult to tally.

As in his previous report on former CIA officers now employed by Google, MacLeod's report on Unit 8200 agents now working in Big Tech identified some prominent examples of these connections, including Gavriel Goidel, Head of Strategy and Operations at Google, who previously served in Unit 8200 to "understand patterns of hostile activists"; Jonathan Cohen, who worked in the role of "team leader" in Unit 8200 from 2000-2003 and has since spent more than thirteen years working in senior positions at Google, where he is currently identified as Head of Insights; and Ben Bariach, a cyber intelligence officer in Unit 8200 from 2007 to 2011, when he commanded "strategic teams of elite officers and professionals," who now serves as a "product partnership manager" at Google.

Using LinkedIn, MacLeod identified "at least 166 former Unit 8200 members" who have gone on to work for Microsoft, including its former Head of Global Strategic Alliances, Ayelet Steinitz; Senior Software Engineer Tomer Lev; and three senior product managers, Maayan Mazig, Or Serok-Jeppa, and Yuval Derman. Based on LinkedIn, it appears that Microsoft is "actively recruiting" from Unit 8200, MacLeod concluded.

The connections between Big Tech companies and US and Israeli intelligence agencies, "highlights the increasing intersection between Silicon Valley and big government," MacLeod concluded in his October 2022 report. Those close ties undermine "any pretense that big tech companies are on our side in the fight to secure and maintain privacy online."

A May 2022 review found no major newspaper coverage of Big Tech companies hiring former US or Israeli intelligence officers as employees. The closest mention came in an October 2021 *Washington Post* article on workers using communications technology to organize, which quoted a former Google employee, Meredith Whittaker, who organized a 2018 walkout, on using Signal and other encrypted communications apps: "Whittaker said secrecy was key to the organizing work at Google because tech employers tend to use surveillance," the *Post* reported, "'They hire ex-CIA folks to surveil,' Whittaker said."[19] Israel's Unit 8200 was mentioned in passing in establishment news coverage of the Pegasus spyware scandal, and the *Wall Street Journal* occasionally quoted former Unit 8200 members as sources on cybersecurity issues.[20] The most prominent US newspapers have not covered Google, Meta, Microsoft, and other Big Tech companies hiring former US and Israeli intelligence officers.

Toxic Chemicals Continue to Go Unregulated in the United States

Neil Bedi, Sharon Lerner, and Kathleen McGrory, "Why the U.S. Is Losing the Fight to Ban Toxic Chemicals," ProPublica, December 14, 2022.

Student Researcher: Reagan Haynie (Loyola Marymount University)

Faculty Evaluator: Mickey Huff (Diablo Valley College)

The United States consistently fails to ban and regulate harmful chemicals, ProPublica reported in December 2022. Neil Bedi, Sharon Lerner, and Kathleen McGrory explained how the Environmental Protection Agency (EPA) and the chemical industry are responsible for causing the United States to become "a global laggard in chemical regulation."

Michal Freedhoff, the EPA's head of chemical regulation, conceded to decades of regulatory failure, blaming the agency's inaction on barriers created by the Trump administration, including funding and staffing shortages. However, ProPublica's investigation revealed broader issues at play. Through interviews with environmental experts and analysis of a half century's worth of legislation, lawsuits, EPA documents, oral histories, chemical databases, and regulatory records, ProPublica uncovered the longstanding institutional failure to protect Americans from toxic chemicals.

Although the 1976 Toxic Substances Control Act (TSCA) gave the EPA regulatory authority to ban or restrict the use of chemicals that pose serious health risks, the chemical industry's involvement in drafting the bill was so extensive that one EPA administrator joked that the law "should have been named after the DuPont executive who went over the text line by line," ProPublica reported. The law required the EPA "to always choose regulations that were the 'least burdensome' to companies. These two words would doom American chemical regulation for decades," Bedi, Lerner, and McGrory wrote.

In 2016, Congress amended the law to remove the "least burdensome" language, but that statute too was seen as "company-friendly." Senator Barbara Boxer (D-CA) stated that the American Chemistry Council (ACC), an industry lobbying group, was an originator of the draft bill, a claim that has been denied by the ACC and a congressional sponsor of the bill, ProPublica reported.

In the meantime, over sixty thousand chemicals remained on the market for years without being vetted for health risks. Some toxins that were originally exempted from regulation include asbestos and trichloroethylene (TCE). ProPublica noted that "asbestos is only one of many toxic substances that are linked to problems like cancers, genetic mutations and fetal harm and that other countries have banned, but the United States has not."

After the 2016 removal of the "least burdensome" language, "the EPA named TCE as one of its 10 high-priority chemicals and tried to propose a ban on high-risk uses that year," according to the ProPublica report. But after industry complaints, the proposal was shelved by the Trump administration, which decided instead to "reassess" TCE. ProPublica noted that in July 2022, the EPA's draft assessment "found that 52 of 54 uses of TCE present an unreasonable risk to human health."

Chemicals are difficult to regulate because the United States still uses a "risk-based" approach in which chemicals are "innocent until proven guilty." This approach "puts the burden on government officials to prove that a chemical poses unreasonable health risks before restricting it," which can take years, ProPublica explained. By contrast, in 2007 the European Union (EU) "switched to a more 'hazard-based' approach, which puts the burden on chemical companies to prove that their products are safe." Under this "no data, no market" approach, the EU has banned or restricted more than a thousand dangerous chemicals.

Another reason for lax US regulations is the burdensome process that encumbers even high-priority chemicals, including asbestos and TCE. Each chemical must undergo a lengthy assessment protocol, but the underfunded EPA cannot keep pace, especially in the face of industry resistance. "The whole regulatory process is designed to be slow and to be slowed down by those opposed to regulation," said Joel Tickner, a leading expert on chemical policy who was interviewed by ProPublica, "Frankly, unless EPA doubled their size, they can't do much with the resources they have."

ProPublica also highlighted industry-friendly staffing practices at the EPA. Specifically, "the EPA has a long history of hiring scientists and top officials from the companies they are supposed to regulate, allowing industry to sway the agency's science from the inside." The revolving door contributes to "the sense that industry science is the best science, which is very much in line with regulators deferring to industry-funded studies showing there isn't cause for concern," said Alissa Cordner, author of *Toxic Safety: Flame Retardants, Chemical Controversies, and Environmental Health*, who was quoted by ProPublica.

In a related story, IFLScience reported in June 2023 on an *Annals of Global Health* study based on decades of secret industry documents about PFAS—so-called "forever chemicals"—showing that "the chemical industry just like the tobacco and oil industries were aware of the dangers of the product they were making but willingly suppressed the knowledge as it would hurt their bottom line."[21] Meanwhile, governments and people pay the price. According to a May 2023 article in DCReport, the global societal costs of PFAS alone are over $17 trillion per year.[22]

A handful of corporate outlets have reported on the EPA's slowness to regulate certain toxic chemicals, including the *Washington Post* and the *New York Times*, occasionally noting business opposition to proposed new rules and the downsides to industry.[23] However, none have highlighted the systemic failures wrought by the EPA and the chemical industry.

Stalkerware Could Be Used to Incriminate People Violating Abortion Bans

Rae Hodge, "With Roe v. Wade Overturned, Your Abortion Searches Could Be Used to Prosecute You," CNET, June 26, 2022.

Danielle Keats Citron, "Abortion Bans Are Going to Make Stalkerware Even More Dangerous," Slate, July 5, 2022.

Student Researcher: David Laskowski (Drew University)

Faculty Evaluator: Lisa Lynch (Drew University)

Stalkerware—surveillance apps that secretly record and upload cellphone activities—could become a significant legal threat to people seeking abortions, according to a pair of articles published in the wake of the US Supreme Court's decision to overturn the constitutional right to abortion. Writing for the tech news site CNET just two days after the *Dobbs* decision, Rae Hodge reported in June 2022 that "already, the digital trails of abortion seekers can become criminal evidence against them in some states where abortion[s] were previously prosecuted. And the legal dangers may extend to abortion seekers in even more states." In her July 2022 article for Slate, University of Virginia law professor Danielle Keats Citron observed that "surveillance accomplished by individual privacy invaders will be a gold mine for prosecutors targeting both medical workers and pregnant people seeking abortions."

Citron explained that cyberstalking software provides users with "real-time access to everything that we do and say with our phones. To do this, they only need our phones (and passwords) for a few minutes. Once installed, cyberstalking apps silently record and upload phones' activities to their servers. They enable privacy invaders to see our photos, videos, texts, calls, voice mails, searches, social media activities, locations—nothing is out of reach. From anywhere, individuals can activate a phone's mic to listen to conversations within 15 feet of the phone."

This could even "include conversations that pregnant people have with their health care providers—nurses, doctors, and insurance company employees," Citron warned. Hodge concurred, "It's not just abortion patients who are at risk of surveillance and arrest. Those who aid abortion seekers could be charged as accomplices in some cases," depending on state law.

Often marketed as a tool to monitor children's online safety or as device trackers, stalkerware is technically illegal to sell for the purpose of monitoring adults but nonetheless is readily available. Citron discovered "more than 200 apps and services that charge subscribers a monthly fee in exchange for providing secret access to people's phones." Stalkerware and other forms of electronic surveillance have been closely associated with domestic violence and sexual assault, according to the National Network to End Domestic Violence, Citron noted.[24]

Stalkerware phone apps are not the only cause for concern. Hodge explained that "third-party data brokers sell sensitive geolocation data—culled through a vast web of personal tracking tech found in apps, browsers and devices—to law enforcement without oversight." Furthermore, the so-called "abortion bounty hunter" provisions adopted by some states, including Texas and Oklahoma, might financially incentivize civilians to use such data to enforce abortion restrictions.[25] "Given the inexpensive cost of readily available stores of personal data and how easily they can be de-anonymized, savvy informants could use the information to identify abortion seekers and turn a profit," Hodge noted.

Even before the *Dobbs* decision, US law has not kept up with the ability of technology to breach individual privacy. Citron explained that "the law's response to intimate privacy violations is inadequate, lacking a clear conception of what intimate privacy is, why its violation is wrongful, and how it inflicts serious harm upon individuals, groups, and society." The bipartisan American Data Privacy and Protection Act is still "slowly inching through Congress" and "is widely thought toothless," according to Hodge.

In July 2022, Emma Woollacott reported for Cybernews that "there are now serious fears that data from period-tracking apps, online searches, text message, and location, for example, could be subpoenaed" in the pursuit of abortion prosecutions.[26] In light of this, two additional bills—the My Body, My Data Act and the Health and Location Data Protection Act of 2022—that would limit the use of reproductive and sexual health data and prevent data brokers from selling health and location data have been introduced in Congress. It is unclear how this legislation would impact law enforcement.

STAT reported in May 2023 on a new rule proposed by the Biden administration to protect "certain health data from being used to prosecute both clinicians and patients. But in the current draft, the rulemaking is designed to reinforce the privacy of reproductive health in states where abortion is legal and does little for those seeking abortion in states where it is illegal."[27]

Corporate news outlets have paid some attention to the use of digital data in abortion-related prosecutions. Several major outlets have published pieces about digital privacy in a post-Roe world, but none have focused specifically on how stalkerware could potentially be used in criminal investigations of suspected abortions.[28]

Certified Rainforest Carbon Offsets Mostly "Worthless"

Patrick Greenfield, "Revealed: More than 90% Of Rainforest Carbon Offsets by Biggest Certifier Are Worthless, Analysis Shows," *The Guardian*, January 18, 2023.

"The Carbon Con," SourceMaterial, January 18, 2023.

Tin Fischer and Hannah Knuth, "Disguised Green" ("Grün Getarnt"), *Die Zeit*, January 18, 2023, updated May 1, 2023.

Sharon Zhang, "Report: 94 Percent of Big Provider's Rainforest Carbon Offsets Don't Cut Carbon," Truthout, January 18, 2023.

Student Researcher: Annie Koruga (Ohlone College)

Faculty Evaluator: Mickey Huff (Diablo Valley College)

About 90 percent of rainforest carbon offsets certified by Verra, the world's largest offset certifier, do not reflect real reductions in emissions, according to reports produced jointly by the *Guardian*, SourceMaterial, and *Die Zeit* in January 2023, with subsequent coverage from Truthout. Verra, which runs the Verified Carbon Standard that has issued more than one billion metric tons worth of carbon offsets, certifies three-fourths of all voluntary carbon offsets.

Overall, the investigative reports found that where Verra claimed to have certified 94.9 million credits—each of which is supposed to represent a one-metric ton reduction of carbon emissions—the actual benefits of the projects validated by Verra amounted to a much more modest 5.5 million credits. To assess the efficacy of Verra's carbon offset certification program, investigative journalists from the *Guardian*, SourceMaterial, and *Die Zeit* analyzed the only three scientific studies to use robust, scientifically sound methods to assess the impact of carbon offsets on deforestation. The journalists also consulted with indigenous communities, industry insiders, and scientists.

The investigation of twenty-nine Verra rainforest offset projects found that twenty-one had no climate benefit, seven had significantly less climate benefit than claimed (by margins of 52 to 98 percent less benefit than claimed), while one project yielded 80 percent more climate benefit than claimed. Overall, the study concluded that 94 percent of the credits approved by these projects were "worthless" and never should have been approved.

Another study conducted by a team of scientists at the University of Cambridge found that in thirty-two of the forty forest offset projects investigated, the claims concerning forest protection and emission reductions were overstated by an average of 400 percent.[29] Despite claims that these thirty-two projects together protected an area of rainforest the size of Italy, they only protected an area the size of Venice. Verra has criticized the studies' conclusions and questioned their methodology.[30]

Several internationally renowned corporations—including Disney, Shell, Gucci, Salesforce, Netflix, and United Airlines, among others—have purchased Verra rainforest carbon credits.

Because Verra sets the standards for offset programs and profits from them, it has an incentive to overstate the climate benefits of carbon offsets. In one project on the shores of Lake Kariba in Zimbabwe, for example, the threat to protected rainforest lands was massively overstated. Project managers on the ground claimed to have originally intended to report that the project would offset fifty-two metric tons of carbon emissions, but Verra instructed them to recalculate the impact, prompting the managers to report that the project would offset 197 million metric tons.

In separate coverage, SourceMaterial reported that a reforestation project in the Republic of the Congo, promoted by the French energy company TotalEnergies, displaced more than four hundred local farmers, some of whom told reporters they received the equivalent of as little as one dollar per hectare in compensation, or nothing at all in some cases, for their land, undermining their livelihoods and local food security in the name of fighting climate change.[31]

The investigations by the *Guardian*, *Die Zeit*, and SourceMaterial appear to have made a difference. In March 2023, Verra announced that it would phase out its flawed rainforest offset program by mid-2025. A senior Verra spokesperson made the announcement "amid growing scrutiny of the carbon offsetting sector's ability to mitigate climate breakdown," according to the *Guardian*, which noted that the multibillion-dollar carbon offset industry is unregulated and, according to insiders, "rife with conflicts of interest."[32]

Nevertheless, establishment news outlets have almost entirely ignored the findings of the joint investigation by the *Guardian, Die Zeit,* and SourceMaterial, while offering a mixed assessment of carbon offset programs more generally. In September 2022, the *Wall Street Journal* reported that "companies looking to offset their emissions are buying credits in vast numbers that do little to help neutralize their carbon output."[33] By contrast, in an October 2022 article on "the bold promises" of carbon offset programs, *Time* described how Verra and other major carbon offset organizations only certify "scientifically sound" projects "with permanent, measurable emissions that are conservatively estimated—meaning the methodology doesn't overestimate the climate benefits of the project."[34] The subsequent investigation by the *Guardian, Die Zeit,* and SourceMaterial casts serious doubt on *Time* magazine's bold assertion.

In January 2023, the *Chicago Tribune* published an editorial that briefly addressed the joint investigation by the *Guardian, Die Zeit,* and SourceMaterial in light of (inaccurate) reports that the federal Consumer Product Safety Commission was preparing to issue a ban on gas stoves.[35] The *Tribune*'s editorial is the only example Project Censored has been able to document of a major US newspaper acknowledging the finding that more than 90 percent of

Verra's certified rainforest offsets are "phantom credits" that "do not represent genuine carbon reductions."

Unions Won More Than 70 Percent of Their Elections in 2022, and Their Victories Are Being Driven by Workers of Color

Mike Elk, "Workers of Color Accounted for 100% of Union Growth in 2022," Payday Report, March 28, 2023.

Marick Masters, "Worker Strikes and Union Elections Surged in 2022—Could It Mark a Turning Point for Organized Labor?" The Conversation, January 5, 2023.

Prem Thakker, "Workers of Color Made Up 100% of Union Growth in 2022," *New Republic*, March 24, 2023.

Andrea Hsu and Alina Selyukh, "Union Wins Made Big News This Year. Here Are 5 Reasons Why It's Not the Full Story," NPR, December 27, 2022.

Student Researchers: Annie Koruga (Ohlone College) and Cem İsmail Addemir (Illinois State University)

Faculty Evaluators: Robin Takahashi (Ohlone College) and Steve Macek (North Central College)

According to reporting by NPR in December 2022 and The Conversation in January 2023, unions won more than 70 percent of their certification elections in 2022. In fiscal year 2022, 2,510 petitions for union representation were filed with the National Labor Relations Board (NLRB) between October 1, 2021, and September 30, 2022.[36] This figure is up 53 percent from FY 2021 when 1,638 petitions were filed. In FY 2022, 1,249 certification elections were held, with workers voting to certify a union as their collective bargaining agent 72 percent of the time.

As Marick Masters explained in his January 2023 article for The Conversation, one business that saw large-scale union activity was Starbucks, with workers holding union elections at 354 stores nationwide, more than a quarter of all US union elections held in 2022. Workers at Starbucks prevailed in four out of every five elections. Workers at Chipotle, Trader Joe's, and Apple unionized for the first time, while workers at Microsoft and Wells Fargo also had wins.

Union activity, Masters reported, most often spikes in times of societal upheaval. From 1934 to 1939, during the Great Depression, the percentage of American workers in a union rose from 7.6 percent to 19.2 percent, and during World War II between 1941 and 1945, from 20 percent to 27 percent. Masters described the current wave of union activity as driven by record levels of economic inequality and continued mobilization of workers in "essential industries," such as healthcare, food, and public safety, who were thrust into harm's way during the global pandemic.

Labor activity—including organizing efforts and strikes—surged in 2022, compared to preceding years. The NLRB tracked twenty large work stoppages that involved more than a thousand workers in 2022, four more than documented in 2021, and 25 percent more than the average number of large work stoppages during the past sixteen years. Since 2021, Cornell University has tracked all labor actions, counting, according to Masters, 385 strikes in 2022, up from 270 in 2021. Moreover, the general public is growing more favorable towards unions. Seventy-one percent of Americans now support unions according to Gallup—a level of support not seen since 1965.[37]

Significantly, the vast majority of recent labor activity is being driven by workers of color. The Bureau of Labor Statistics (BLS) recorded a substantial rise of two hundred thousand unionized workers in the United States from 2021 to 2022, most of whom are workers of color, Prem Thakker reported for the *New Republic*. According to BLS, unionized workers of color increased by 231,000 last year, while White unionized workers decreased by thirty-one thousand. Recent data shows that the largest increase in union membership in 2022 occurred in state and local government positions in the South. Low-wage workers of color in the public sector have been driving the overall gains.

Thakker noted that, according to BLS data, "industries that saw the largest increases in unionization were state government; durable goods manufacturing; arts, entertainment, and recreation; and transportation and warehousing." States with the largest increases in unionization included California, Texas, Ohio, Maryland, and Alabama. Whereas Republican and Democratic politicians often separate concerns over working conditions and pay from issues of identity, these data demonstrate how identity and workers' rights are closely connected. "After all, unionization and labor struggles are direct mechanisms to better accomplish racial and social equality; the ability for people to afford to live happy and dignified lives is inherently tied to their ability to enjoy fundamental social and civil rights within those lives, too," Thakker wrote.

Despite recent inroads at employers like Starbucks and growing popular support for unions, the power of organized labor is nowhere close to what it once was. As Masters pointed out, more than a third of workers were unionized in the 1950s, whereas only a tenth were in 2021. Before the 1980s, there were typically more than five thousand union elections in any given year, and as recently as 1980, there were two hundred major work stoppages.

Corporate media coverage of the labor resurgence of 2022 was highly selective and, in some ways, misleading. The establishment press has published hundreds of articles on union organizing at corporations such as Starbucks and Amazon and among graduate students at universities across the country. Yahoo republished Masters's The Conversation article about union success in elections, and Vox, Bloomberg Law, and the *Washington Post* all remarked on organized labor's recent string of certification vote victories.[38] Yet corporate coverage of current labor organizing often fails to address the outsized role played by workers of color in union growth, the sectors and geographic areas where unions are adding members, and the shrinking number of White workers represented by collective bargaining agents.

Moreover, corporate coverage of recent union successes has rarely placed them in a proper historical context. One exception was a January 2022 article in the *New York Times* which reported that, despite the growing popularity of unions, high-profile organizing campaigns at Starbucks and Amazon, and the significant involvement of women in union activities, there has been a pronounced downward trend in union membership during the past forty years.[39]

The article even quoted a labor studies professor, Ruth Milkman, who attributed the decline in union membership to private employers' heavy-handed efforts to undermine organizing campaigns and labor laws that strongly favor employers.

Fossil Fuel Investors Sue Governments to Block Climate Regulations

Rishika Pardikar, "Big Oil Is Suing Countries to Block Climate Action," The Lever, June 8, 2022.

Lois Parshley, "The Secretive Legal Weapon That Fossil Fuel Interests Use Against Climate-Conscious Countries," Grist, January 17, 2023.

Kyla Tienhaara et al., "Investor-State Disputes Threaten the Global Green Energy Transition," *Science* 376, no. 6594 (May 5, 2022): 701-03.

Student Researcher: Reagan Haynie (Loyola Marymount University)

Faculty Evaluator: Mickey Huff (Diablo Valley College)

Big oil companies and their investors are suing governments to thwart climate change policies, Rishika Pardikar reported for The Lever in June 2022. These fossil fuel stakeholders claim that laws designed to address climate change are undermining their profits—and, therefore, that they must be compensated for any resulting financial losses. According to Pardikar, "such moves could have a chilling effect on countries' ability to take climate action" because of the fear and uncertainty they cause.

One case featuring Vermilion, a Canadian oil and gas company, demonstrates how investor threats are making it difficult for countries to act against climate change. As described in Pardikar's article, in 2017, France's environmental minister at the time, Nicolas Hulot, drafted a law to end fossil fuel extraction by 2040. In response, the Canadian oil company threatened to use an "investor-state dispute settlement" (ISDS) to sue the French government, thus taking advantage of a provision that allows investors to sue governments for treaty violations. Due to the ISDS, Hulot's climate change bill was diluted, enabling oil and gas companies to continue extraction after the originally approved 2040 deadline.

Other reports citing ISDS actions indicated that these efforts consistently benefit fossil fuel companies and their investors. Lea Di Salvatore's 2021 inquiry into climate-related ISDS reports for the International Institute for Sustainable Development found that fossil fuel investors won their settlements 72 percent of the time.[40] This resulted in fossil fuel investors being awarded more than $600 million in compensation.

The situation has only gotten worse since fifty countries, most of them in Europe, enacted the Energy Charter Treaty (ECT). Pardikar cited specific articles from the ECT that call for "fair and equitable treatment" of investors and "payment of prompt, adequate and effective compensation." Additionally, in instances where governments obtain investor assets, investors can invoke clauses in the ECT to threaten legal action against lawmakers for future climate proposals.

The European Union (EU) recently attempted to push back by "revising" the ECT to account for climate goals. However, as The Lever reported, European Parliament Chairman Pascal Canfin announced that mediation efforts failed, and the ECT will likely "continue to be used by investors to sue states taking climate action." Consequently, the chairman called on all EU countries to exit the Energy Charter Treaty.

Many climate activists and lawmakers are concerned that the ISDS system will prompt future actions against climate progress. Laura Létourneau-Tremblay, an international investment law researcher at the University of Oslo, explained that ISDS provisions requiring states to compensate fossil fuel companies could "prevent governments from taking ambitious climate actions." Létourneau-Tremblay told The Lever, there are "real concerns as to whether the ECT is compatible with the net-zero energy transition."

Shortly after President Biden revoked the Keystone Pipeline permits in January 2021, the Canadian company TC Energy took legal action against the US government. The company filed a lawsuit, citing a "responsibility to our shareholders to seek recovery of the losses incurred due to the permit revocation." TC Energy won and was awarded $15 billion in damages.

One of the most concerning aspects of the ISDS is that it offers foreign companies a loophole allowing them to avoid local courts—which frequently operate under stricter regulations. Instead, suits brought by companies against countries in which they have investments are decided by international arbitration tribunals, which are notoriously lacking in transparency. Moreover, under

ISDS rules nations cannot file suits against foreign companies, they can only react to claims filed against them.

Grist published an article on the topic in January 2023, more than a year after Di Salvatore's report for the International Institute for Sustainable Development. The Independent also reported on fossil fuel companies suing governments, mentioning the ISDS and specific countries that have faced lawsuits (such as Italy and Slovenia).[41] However, it only briefly touched on the concern that these lawsuits could prevent climate action. Beyond this handful of reports, the topic has received little coverage from major news outlets.

Proximity to Oil and Gas Extraction Sites Linked to Maternal Health Risks and Childhood Leukemia

Nick Cunningham, "Living Close to Oil and Gas Drilling Linked to Higher Risk of Pregnancy Complications, New Study Finds," DeSmog, January 11, 2022.

Nick Cunningham, "Children Living Close to Fracking Sites Have Two to Three Times Higher Risk of Leukemia," DeSmog, August 17, 2022.

Tom Perkins, "Children Born Near Fracking Wells More at Risk for Leukemia— Study," *The Guardian*, August 17, 2022.

Student Researchers: Grace Engel (Salisbury University) and Ashley Rogers (Drew University)

Faculty Evaluators: Jennifer Cox (Salisbury University) and Lisa Lynch (Drew University)

Two epidemiological studies, from 2021 and 2022, provide new evidence that living near oil and gas extraction sites is hazardous to human health, especially for pregnant mothers and children, as reported by Nick Cunningham for DeSmog and Tom Perkins for the *Guardian*.

Researchers from Oregon State University (OSU) measured the effects of oil- and gas-drilling sites on the health of pregnant women living within six miles of drilling operations during a thirteen-year period. The study, reported in DeSmog in January 2022, was the first that specifically examined the impacts of oil and gas drilling on hypertension in pregnant women.[42]

Based on data for more than 2.8 million pregnant women living in Texas between 1996 to 2009, the OSU researchers found that pregnant women living within one kilometer (~0.6 miles) of a drilling site had a 5 percent greater likelihood of gestational hypertension and a 26 percent higher risk of eclampsia, a rare but serious condition where high blood pressure results in seizures during pregnancy, than pregnant mothers living further from drilling sites. Oil- and gas-drilling sites contaminate water, pollute the air, and produce noise pollution. These consequences of drilling likely increase stress among expecting mothers, contributing to gestational hypertension and eclampsia. The researchers controlled for a variety of potential confounding factors, including household income and proximity to the nearest highway.

Notably, the data in the OSU study predate the widespread development of "fracking," or hydraulic fracturing, the process of extracting gas and oil from shale beds by injecting fluids at high pressure. Although much research has focused on the negative impacts of fracking, the OSU study shows how more conventional forms of oil and gas extraction impact pregnant women and their babies.[43]

A Yale University study, reported by DeSmog and the *Guardian* in August 2022, found that children who resided in areas bordering fracking sites were two to three times more likely to develop acute lymphoblastic leukemia (ALL), a type of blood cancer. The study, published in the journal *Environmental Health Perspectives*, involved 405 children aged 2–7 diagnosed with ALL in Pennsylvania between 2009–2017, who were compared with an additional 2,080 children, matched on birth year, who did not have leukemia.[44] The researchers found that children residing less than two kilometers (approximately 1.2 miles) from a fracking site were much more likely to develop leukemia, having been exposed to toxins such as radioactive debris, particle pollution, and contaminated water.

Noting that Pennsylvania requires only 500-foot setbacks, while other states have requirements as low as 150 feet, the *Guardian* reported that the publication of the Yale study coincided with "debate over how far wells should be set from residences." The fossil fuel industry has fought to block any expanded setback requirements. Based on the study's findings, one of the authors, Cassie Clark, told the *Guardian* that existing setback distances are "insufficiently protective of children's health."

As of this volume's publication, no major US newspapers appear to have covered the Oregon State University study on gestational hypertension and eclampsia in mothers living near oil- and gas-drilling sites or the Yale University study on links between acute lymphoblastic leukemia in children and proximity to fracking sites. *Smithsonian* magazine, The Hill, and WHYY, an NPR affiliate serving the Philadelphia region, covered the fracking study.[45] In June 2022, *U.S. News & World Report* published an article on the states most threatened by oil and gas production, which noted that "more than 17 million people, including nearly 4 million children, live within a half-mile radius" of active oil and gas production facilities but did not mention either the OSU or Yale studies.[46]

Deadly Decade for Environmental Activists

Patrick Greenfield, "More Than 1,700 Environmental Activists Murdered in the Past Decade— Report," *The Guardian*, September 28, 2022.

Stuti Mishra, "Over 1,700 Environmental Activists Murdered in 10 Years, Investigation Finds," Independent, September 29, 2022.

Matt McGrath, "Over 1,700 Environment Activists Killed in Decade— Report," BBC, September 29, 2022.

Joseph Lee, "Every Two Days, a Land Defender Is Killed. Most Are Indigenous," Grist, September 30, 2022.

Matt Alderton, "NGO Reports 'Deadly Decade' for Environmental Defenders," TreeHugger, October 12, 2022.

Student Researcher: Annie Koruga (Ohlone College)

Faculty Evaluator: Robin Takahashi (Ohlone College)

Independent reporting in Fall 2022 revealed that, between 2012 and 2021, at least 1,733 environmental activists were killed—amounting, on average, to nearly one killing every two days across ten years. This figure from the Global Witness study, *Decade of Defiance*, is "almost certainly an underestimate" because "conflict, restrictions on a free press and civil society, and lack of independent monitoring of attacks on defenders can lead to underreporting," Global Witness asserted.[47]

The killing of environmental activists has been concentrated in the Global South, with 68 percent occurring in Latin America. Three-hundred-forty-two killings occurred in Brazil, 322 in Colombia, 154 in Mexico, 177 in Honduras, and eighty in Guatemala. Outside Latin America, the Philippines accounted for 270 killings and India accounted for seventy-nine.

Indigenous land defenders are disproportionately impacted. *The Guardian* reported that 39 percent of those killed were from Indigenous communities, despite that group constituting only 5 percent of the global population. In Brazil, about a third of those killed were Indigenous or Afro-descendants, and in the Philippines, that number was about 40 percent. Additionally, 85 percent of the killings in Brazil occurred in the Amazon rainforest.[48]

Grist's report on the Global Witness study quoted Dinamam Tuxá of the Articulation of Indigenous Peoples of Brazil (APIB), Brazil's largest coalition of Indigenous groups: "There has been an increase in the amount of conflict—socio and environmental conflict—in our lands," Tuxá told Grist, "It's destroying communities and it's destroying our forests."

Although most of these killings cannot be traced to a specific cause, the Independent explained that a "big proportion of these attacks" are associated with opposition to "mining and infrastructure, including large-scale agribusiness and hydroelectric dams." In 2021 alone, twenty-seven killings were linked to mining, thirteen to hydropower, five to agribusiness, four to roads and infrastructure, and four to logging. In total, Global Witness documented two hundred killings in 2021, down slightly from the 227 verified the previous year.

Threats to environmental activists are not limited to killings. Environmental activists also face beatings, arbitrary arrests and detention, strategic lawsuits against public participation (SLAPPs) brought by companies, sexual violence, and surveillance. A separate April 2022 report from the Business and Human Rights Resource Centre, as reported by Grist, documented more than 3,800 attacks on human rights defenders—including not only killings and death threats but also beatings, arbitrary arrests and detention, and lawsuits—between January 2015 and March 2021. Grist noted that many of these human rights defenders were "known in particular for defending their communities' natural resources from mining, deforestation, water contamination, and other threats."[49]

Those who kill, injure, detain, or harass environmental activists often do so with impunity, due to insufficient or nonexistent criminal investigations, corruption, and intimidation. Nevertheless, the BBC reported that in Honduras a former energy executive was sentenced to twenty-two years in prison for the 2016 murder of activist Berta Cáceres. In 2021, the Escazú Agreement—the first human rights and environmental treaty in Latin America and the Caribbean—also went into effect. Mexico has ratified the agreement, but Brazil and Colombia have not.

In September 2022, the *New York Times* published an article by Oscar Lopez, reporting how Mexico was deemed the deadliest country for environmental activists by Global Witness.[50] In October 2022, a short piece in the *New York Times*'s climate newsletter "Climate Forward" about why Latin America is so dangerous for environmental activists also cited Global Witness's report.[51] And on February 26, 2023, the *Los Angeles Times* published an op-ed by Rafael Lozano and Anjan Sundaram about attacks on Mexican Indigenous communities fighting climate change that referenced Global Witness's findings.[52] Otherwise, the corporate media have largely ignored the Global Witness study about the deadly wave of assaults on environmentalists during the past decade.

Project Censored previously covered the 2014 edition of Global Witness's report on the killing of environmental activists, *Deadly Environment*, which was also significantly under-reported by establishment news outlets in the United States.[53]

Corporate Profits Hit Record High as Top 0.1% Earnings and Wall Street Bonuses Skyrocket

Jake Johnson, "'All of Us Are Paying the Price' as Corporate Profits Surge to Record-High $2 Trillion," Common Dreams, August 26, 2022; republished as "Corporate Profits Surge to an All-Time High of $2 Trillion," Truthout, August 26, 2022.

Jake Johnson, "Fueling Inequality, Earnings of Top 0.1% in US Have Soared by 465% Since 1979: Analysis," Common Dreams, December 21, 2022

Jessica Corbett, "Price Gouging at the Pump Results in 235% Profit Jump for Big Oil: Analysis," Common Dreams, July 29, 2022.

Jake Johnson, "'Jaw-Dropping': Wall Street Bonuses Have Soared 1,743% Since 1985," Common Dreams, March 23, 2022.

Student Researcher: Annie Koruga (Ohlone College)

Faculty Evaluator: Robin Takahashi (Ohlone College)

Corporate profits rose to an "all-time high" in 2022, producing an explosion in income for the very wealthy, Jake Johnson reported for Common Dreams in a series of 2022 articles. In August 2022, Johnson explained that non-financial corporate profits in the second quarter of 2022 hit two trillion dollars, an increase of 8.1 percent from the same period in 2021 and their highest level since 1950. In December 2022, Johnson reported on research by the Economic Policy Institute (EPI) that showed the earnings of the wealthiest 0.1 percent in the United States grew by 465 percent between 1979 and 2021 while the income of the bottom 90 percent grew less than 29 percent.[54]

One reason profits are booming is that companies have been using inflation as cover to raise prices and gouge consumers. In late 2022, inflation in the United States was the highest it had been in forty years. According to Rakeen Mabud, chief economist at the Groundwork Collaborative, "Astronomical corporate profits confirm what corporate executives have been telling us on earning calls over and over again: They're making a lot of money by charging people more, and they don't plan on bringing prices down anytime soon."

The fossil fuel industry has enjoyed especially lavish profits. As Jessica Corbett reported for Common Dreams in July 2022, the eight largest oil companies' profits spiked 235 percent between the second quarter of 2021 and the second quarter of 2022, resulting in a combined $52 billion profit, according to an analysis by Accountable.US.[55] Exxon-Mobil profited $17.85 billion; Chevron, $11.62 billion; and Shell, $11.47 billion. Notably, in 2021-2022, the oil and gas industry spent more than $200 million lobbying Congress to oppose climate action.

As Johnson reported in December 2022, the main beneficiaries of big corporations' windfall profits have been the ultrarich. He cited EPI data showing that the average income of someone in the bottom 90 percent of the workforce in 2021 was $36,571, while the average income of the wealthiest 0.1 percent that same year was $3,312,693, or more than ninety times as much. In 1979, this discrepancy was not nearly so great, with someone in the bottom 90 percent earning $28,415, while the average individual in the top 0.1 percent earned $586,222, or 20.6 times as much. As of 2021, the share of wealth earned by the 0.1 percent had hit a historic high, while the wealth of the bottom 90 percent had sunk to a record low.

The very rich—billionaires and multimillionaires—are getting wealthier at a faster rate than even the merely wealthy. The top 0.1 percent made about 1.6 percent of all annual earnings in 1979, but by 2021, that share had increased to 5.9 percent, more than tripling the slice of the total national income captured by the ultrarich.

Bloated bonuses for Wall Street bankers and stockbrokers added to the enormous sums being raked in by the rich in 2020 and 2021. In March 2022, Johnson reported on an analysis by Inequality.org of New York State Comptroller data that found the average bonus for Wall Street employees rose an astounding 1,743 percent between 1985 and 2021.[56] In 2021 alone, Wall Street bonuses grew 20 percent, far outpacing inflation at 7 percent, and nominal private sector earnings at 4.2 percent. That year Wall Street bonuses, in aggregate, amounted to $45 billion, the highest since 2006.[57] Had the minimum wage increased at the same rate as Wall Street bonuses, it would now be $61.75 per hour.

The establishment media have reported intermittently on record corporate profits, but this coverage has tended to downplay corporate use of inflation as a pretext for hiking prices. In August 2022, for example, Bloomberg observed that "a measure of US profit margins has reached its widest since 1950," but its report did not mention the two trillion dollar figure.[58] In June 2022, ABC News aired a rare package examining the debate among economists over whether "elevated corporate profits" might be contributing to inflation.[59] The same month the *New York Times* published a lengthy article on the disagreement among economists about the relationship of corporate profits to "greedflation." The *Times* quoted experts from EPI and Groundwork Collaborative but refused to draw any firm conclusions.[60]

The EPI study on the accelerating incomes of the ultrarich was virtually ignored by the corporate media, although Insider referenced it in a story about how a coming recession might hurt the wealthy most.[61]

Establishment press coverage of the massive bonuses awarded to Wall Street employees in 2021 has been scant. Reuters ran a story on it, as did the *New York Post*.[62] CNN Business noted that "high bonuses are also good news for Gotham's tax coffers."[63]

Tribal Towns Forced to Relocate
Due to Climate Crisis

Alex Lubben et al., "These Communities Are Trapped in Harm's Way as Climate Disasters Mount," *Mother Jones*, August 4, 2022.

Emily Schwing, "Interior Department Puts $40m Toward Community Relocation Efforts for Newtok and Napakiak," Alaska Public Media, December 2, 2022.

Emily Schwing, "Newtok Residents Are Desperate to Relocate after September Storm," Alaska Public Media, October 4, 2022.

Emily Schwing, "How Far Can $25 Million Go to Relocate a Community That's Disappearing into Alaska's Melting Permafrost?" *High Country News*, January 18, 2023.

Student Researcher: Jette-Mari Stammer (North Central College)

Faculty Evaluator: Steve Macek (North Central College)

Many coastal areas in the Pacific Northwest lose up to seventy feet of their land annually due to erosion caused by climate change, disproportionately impacting the region's Indigenous communities. The Biden administration has already paid $25 million apiece to three Native American villages in Alaska and Washington to move away from the encroaching waters, a first managed retreat for Indigenous communities in the country, with many more to come. However, the aid that has been allocated will not even cover the cost of building new schools, according to a series of December 2022 reports by Emily Schwing for Alaska Public Media and *High Country News*.

Managed retreats are disruptive and relocating communities must overcome a host of challenges, from choosing new locations to securing funds from the Interior Department and other federal agencies. Unfortunately, such relocations are likely to become more common as flooding and erosion affect a growing number of coastal Indigenous communities.

The first communities to receive the $25 million federal disbursements were Newtok, in southwest Alaska; Napakiak, on the shore of the Kuskokwim River; and the Quinault Indian Nation, on Washington state's Olympic Peninsula.

In the case of Newtok, at least fifty-four houses, an airport, a power grid, and a road system will need to be built at an estimated cost of $120-300 million. Constructing a new sewage system and a health clinic would add an estimated $105 million to the price of relocation.

Navigating the bureaucratic rules that dictate how funding can be used makes the task of moving a village even more daunting. The Newtok relocation project manager, Patrick LeMay, told *High Country News* that, according to the Department of the Interior, funding is "supposed to support core infrastructure. But the Bureau of Indian Affairs—which is part of the Interior Department—does not consider housing infrastructure." The rest of the money must be scraped together from different agencies with their own requirements.

An August 2022 report by Columbia Journalism Investigations and the Center for Public Integrity published in *Mother Jones* revealed that people of color make up more than 50 percent of residents living in counties that have experienced three climate disasters in the past five years. The same report highlighted that the Federal Emergency Management Agency's "disaster preparedness spending—which includes money to help people relocate—already falls short of the need" and is "not flowing out equitably."

Journalist Emily Schwing has provided the most detailed account of the Alaska relocations. Together with the *Mother Jones* article on the federal government's lack of preparedness, her reports for public and independent media outlets document the inadequacy of the federal government's spending on climate-related relocations. While the *New York Times*, CNBC, and The Hill all covered the Biden administration's initial allocation of funding to the three Native American towns, these outlets failed to explore the full scope of the relocations' impacts and often omitted the perspectives of community leaders on the daunting bureaucratic obstacles tribes encounter trying to access government funding.[64]

Fossil Fuel Money Skews University Climate and Energy Research

Oliver Milman, "Exxon in the Classroom: How Big Oil Money Influences US Universities," *The Guardian*, March 27, 2023.

Abby Saks and Phoebe Barr, "Fossil Fuel Companies Are Donating Millions to Skew University Research," *The Nation*, March 30, 2023.

Amy Westervelt, "Fossil Fuel Companies Donated $700m to US Universities Over 10 Years," *The Guardian*, March 1, 2023.

Student Researcher: Angel Kifer (Frostburg State University)

Faculty Evaluator: Andy Duncan (Frostburg State University)

Fossil fuel companies have been donating millions of dollars to US universities for climate and energy research projects, according to reports published in March 2023 by the *Guardian* and *The Nation*, based on a study produced by Data for Progress, a progressive think tank.[65] Fossil fuel funding, *The Nation* reported, aims to "skew the results, timing, and presentation of scientific research."

Even as Princeton University announced in September 2022 that it would divest from fossil fuels, dozens of universities in the United States continue to accept millions of dollars from ExxonMobil, BP, Chevron, Shell, ConocoPhillips, and allied interests, such as Koch Industries, to fund climate and energy research. Based on its examination of twenty-seven universities that together received more than $667 million in fossil fuel donations or pledges between 2010 and 2020, Data for Progress reported that the top recipients of fossil fuel funding were the University of California, Berkeley; the University of Illinois Urbana-Champaign; George Mason University; Stanford; the University of Texas at Austin; MIT; Princeton; Rice; Texas A&M; and Harvard. UC Berkeley alone accepted $154 million during the 2010s.

"Fossil-fuel firms have purposely sought to 'colonize' academia with industry-friendly science, rather than seed overt climate denial," the *Guardian* reported on March 27, 2023, quoting Ben Franta, a senior research fellow at the University of Oxford who studies the industry's influence on universities. In its March 1, 2023, report, the *Guardian* quoted Bella Kumar, the lead author of the Data for Progress study: "These research projects have real-life implications," Kumar stated, noting, for example, that "fossil fuel-funded research has re-centered natural gas in the conversation about renewables."

Although the *Guardian* and *The Nation* helped focus public attention on the issue, the nation's most prominent newspapers have reported it only fitfully, with the strongest accounts appearing as opinion articles or relegated to online content.[66] A May 2023 report by CBS News directly addressed the Data for Progress study, stating that "many schools, including Stanford University in Palo Alto, California, accept donations from oil and gas companies to support climate change research."[67] However, CBS News emphasized student efforts to encourage divestment, and, in contrast with the *Guardian*'s coverage, its report did little to illuminate how funding from Big Oil and its allies promotes industry-friendly research, rather than overt climate denial.

Project Censored has previously covered problems with fossil fuel companies funding university research, noting in its 2018 yearbook that corporate news media rarely discussed the subject.[68] It would appear that little has changed.

Accidents Reveal US Biolab Vulnerabilities

Mara Hvistendahl, "Bent Over in Pain," The Intercept, November 1, 2022.

Student Researcher: Reagan Haynie (Loyola Marymount University)

Faculty Evaluator: Mickey Huff (Diablo Valley College)

The Intercept's Mara Hvistendahl uncovered hundreds of undisclosed accidents at biolabs in the United States. Her November 1, 2022, article spotlighted the case of a graduate student at Washington University School of Medicine in St. Louis, Missouri, who contracted the debilitating Chikungunya virus, which is responsible for epidemics in both the Caribbean and Africa.

According to Hvistendahl, the graduate student contracted the virus when her syringe slipped and pricked through her gloves. Seeing no blood, she did not initially report the incident. She became ill several days later and tested positive for Chikungunya. Because she did not report the incident immediately, no safety measures were put into place following her possible exposure. Her supervisor did ultimately report the accident to the National Institutes of Health (NIH), "but until now, the event has remained out of public view. So have hundreds of other incidents in US labs," Hvistendahl reported.

Accidents like these are not uncommon in US biolabs. The Intercept analyzed more than 5,500 pages of documents from the NIH to reveal a range of issues. Some included "malfunctioning equipment, spilled beakers, transgenic rodents running down the hall, [and] a sedated macaque coming back to life and biting a researcher." Most of the incidents involved minor pathogens or did not lead to infection or illness. However, some accidents did result in illness, such as the Chikungunya incident.

The public often assumes that biolab accidents in the US are rare, but the NIH documents obtained by the Intercept prove otherwise. Hvistendahl explained that "the United States has a patchwork of regulations and guidelines covering lab biosafety. Safety training can vary widely from one institution to the next. Experiments involving specific pathogens and some research funded by the US government are subject to oversight, but critics liken other areas to 'the Wild West,'" Hvistendahl reported, "Unless they work with the most dangerous pathogens, biolabs do not have to register with the US government. As a result, there is little visibility into the biosafety of experiments carried out by private companies or foundations."

In the wake of the claim that the COVID-19 pandemic originated from a lab leak, the corporate media have investigated biolab threats, primarily in other countries.[69] An April 2023 article in the *Washington Post* highlighting Chinese biolabs acknowledged, "Lab accidents happen everywhere, including in the United States, where illnesses and deaths caused by accidental infections have occurred, especially before the adoption of modern safety standards."[70] In May 2023, the *New York Times* featured an opinion article about a new book on biolab threats by investigative journalist Alison Young, who penned an editorial for the *Guardian*.[71] However, corporate coverage has primarily focused on global threats and downplayed the vulnerabilities of biolabs in the United States.

Study Exposes Electric Utilities' Climate Disinformation Campaigns

Robinson Meyer, "It Wasn't Just Oil Companies Spreading Climate Denial," *The Atlantic*, September 7, 2022.

Zoya Teirstein, "America's Electric Utilities Spent Decades Spreading Climate Misinformation," Grist, September 7, 2022; republished by WhoWhatWhy, September 14, 2022.

Student Researcher: Reyna Oliva (North Central College)

Faculty Evaluator: Steve Macek (North Central College)

Electric utility companies have been knowingly spreading disinformation about climate change for decades, Grist and the *Atlantic* reported in September 2022, citing a report published earlier that month in *Environmental Research Letters*. According to this report, electric utility companies, research groups, and trade associations (including the Edison Electric Institute and the Electric Power Research Institute) have been aware of climate change and its effects since the 1960s but neglected to inform the public in order to pursue their own financial gains, thus contributing to "climate denial, doubt, and delay."[72] However, unlike fossil fuel companies, which have long been subject to criticism for employing comparable tactics to downplay the issue of climate change, utility companies and their trade associations have largely escaped scrutiny.

Nevertheless, researchers at the University of California, Santa Barbara, have analyzed nearly two hundred utility industry documents spanning five decades—from 1968 to 2019—which reveal that companies such as PG&E and Commonwealth Edison were perfectly aware of the threats posed by climate change but disregarded them. In fact, electric utility representatives went so far as to dismiss action to reduce carbon emissions as "premature at best." For this reason, one of the study's authors, Leah Stokes, said, "Utilities hold partial responsibility for today's climate crisis, and for the pushback against policies to address it."

The dissemination of climate disinformation is even more serious than what meets the eye. According to the *Environmental Research Letters* article, "climate denial, doubt, and delay have proven profitable" for electric utilities, "allowing them to invest in polluting infrastructure for several decades longer than scientists have advised is safe." The main reason for the many years of apparent deceit surrounding the climate crisis was financial profit, the study's authors reported. One example of the industry's attempts to deny responsibility for climate change was the series of ads created in the 1970s and 1980s that "acknowledged the link between sulfur dioxide and acid rain, yet misleadingly argued that pollution control technologies were infeasible and unnecessary."

The *Environmental Research Letters* article also highlighted connections between industry associations and the American Legislative Exchange Council (ALEC), the Utility Air Regulation Group, and America's Power, each of which has lobbied against climate legislation. "Notably," the authors of the study wrote, "the ten utilities most extensively involved in climate denial stand out as the largest polluters in the industry today."

Although several of the nation's most prominent

newspapers have reported on past studies published in *Environmental Research Letters* about climate denial campaigns by ExxonMobil and other fossil fuel companies, as of May 2023, none of them appear to have covered the efforts of electric utilities to downplay or deny the human causes of climate change.[73]

Black Americans Seven Times More Likely Than Whites to Be Wrongfully Convicted of Serious Crimes

"New Report Highlights Persistent Racial Disparities Among Wrongful Convictions," Innocence Project, September 27, 2022.

Hassan Kanu, "Rising Number of False Convictions Shows Stark Racial Patterns," Reuters, September 27, 2022.

Melissa Noel, "Study: Black Americans More Likely To Be Wrongfully Convicted," *Essence*, September 29, 2022.

Student Researcher: Annie Koruga (Ohlone College)

Faculty Evaluator: Mickey Huff (Diablo Valley College)

As reported by the Innocence Project, Reuters, and *Essence*, a September 2022 National Registry of Exonerations study found that Black people are seven times more likely than White people to be wrongfully convicted of murder, sexual crimes, and drug crimes.

The NRE study analyzed 3,200 exonerations for the above crimes, dating back to 1989.[74] Fifty-three percent of those exonerated were Black, even though Black Americans make up only 13.6 percent of the general population. Only 33 percent of those exonerated were White. Black Americans were 7.5 times more likely than Whites to be wrongly convicted of murder, eight times more likely to be wrongly convicted of sexual crimes, and nineteen times more likely to be wrongly convicted of drug crimes, the Innocence Project reported.

The enormous disparity in wrongful convictions for drug crimes can be explained, in part, by the implicit racial bias of police officers. Police officers investigating drug crimes have broad discretion about whom to search, interrogate, and arrest. In most cases, officers are more likely to identify Black people as suspects. Additionally, the disparity in wrongful rape convictions can often be blamed on White people's misidentification of Black men. Melissa Noel's article for *Essence* quoted from the National Registry of Exonerations report: "A substantial number of the convictions that led to rape exonerations of Black defendants were marred by implicit biases, racially tainted official misconduct and, in some cases, explicit racism."

Unfortunately, this systematic disparity has grown slightly in recent years. In 2017, the National Registry of Exonerations published a similar report which found Black Americans were seven times more likely than White Americans to be wrongfully convicted of murder, a number that has since grown to 7.5 times more likely.

These findings have received minimal corporate media coverage. Christina Swarns, executive director of the

Innocence Project, wrote an op-ed for the *Los Angeles Times* on the National Registry report.[75] An article published by ABC News in March 2023 also referenced statistics from the study.[76]

Municipalities in Puerto Rico Sue Fossil Fuel Giants Under Organized Crime Law

Kenny Stancil, "Puerto Rican Towns File RICO Suit Accusing Big Oil of Colluding on Climate Denial," Common Dreams, November 29, 2022.

Clark Mindock, "Puerto Rican Towns Sue Big Oil Under Rico Alleging Collusion on Climate Denial," Reuters, November 29, 2022.

Joe Wilkins, "Puerto Rico's Electricity Nightmare Was Brought to You by Privatization," *Jacobin*, October 6, 2022.

Ryan Cooper, "Puerto Rico's Colonial State Left It Vulnerable to Hurricane Fiona," *American Prospect*, September 23, 2022.

Student Researcher: Vikki Vasquez (California State University, East Bay)

Faculty Evaluator: Mickey Huff (Diablo Valley College)

Sixteen municipalities in Puerto Rico are suing Chevron, ExxonMobil, Shell, and other fossil fuel companies for their efforts to deny the role of fossil fuels in causing climate change. In a November 2022 report for Common Dreams, Kenny Stancil described the case as a "first of its kind" racketeering lawsuit that seeks to hold the fossil fuel corporations financially responsible for the damages caused by the hurricanes that devastated Puerto Rico in 2017. *Municipalities of Bayamon et al. v. Exxon Mobil Corp. et al.* contends that the 2017 hurricane season was made worse by global warming and that fossil fuel companies colluded to deceive the public about the impact of fossil fuel products on the climate.

Although dozens of US municipalities and states have attempted to sue fossil fuel corporations for climate change-related damages, the class action suit filed by Puerto Rican municipalities is the first to do so under RICO, the Racketeer Influenced and Corrupt Organizations Act, established in 1970, to enhance the control of organized crime.

The lawsuit contends that ExxonMobil, Shell, and others colluded to deceive consumers through a "fraudulent marketing scheme" intended to convince the public that fossil fuel products do not alter the climate. As Reuters reported, the lawsuit alleges that the companies' coordinated deception, undertaken over decades, violated US racketeering and antitrust laws.

The 2017 hurricane season caused more than $294 billion in damages in Puerto Rico, according to the lawsuit. Beyond catastrophic damage to critical infrastructure, including healthcare and educational facilities, two of the hurricanes, Irma and Maria, caused an estimated 4,600 deaths. A partner at one of the law firms representing the municipalities, Marc Grossman, called Puerto Rico "the ultimate victim of global warming."

Hurricane Maria, which hit Puerto Rico in September 2017, resulted in an island-wide blackout and paved the way for the island's power grid to be completely privatized by LUMA Energy, a joint venture owned by the Canadian firm ATCO and US contractor Quanta Services, Stancil reported.

An October 2022 report in *Jacobin* by Joe Wilkins described how LUMA Energy was able to capitalize on Puerto Rico's misfortune. In 2016, the US Congress passed the Puerto Rico Oversight, Management, and Economic Stability Act, which allowed the US government to exert influence on Puerto Rico's finances through the Financial Oversight and Management Board (FOMB). As Wilkins explained, the United States pressured Puerto Rico to cut public services to "achieve fiscal responsibility" while also denying unions the right to strike. "The FOMB's independence from Puerto Rican lawmakers meant that it could clear the way for Puerto Rico's public electrical company, the Puerto Rico Electric Power Authority (PREPA), to sell commonwealth assets and outsource services related to the generation and transfer of electricity," Wilkins wrote. After the devastating 2017 hurricane season, privatization was pitched as the solution to the island's outdated electrical grid.

Although Reuters covered the story, as of May 2023, no major US corporate news outlets appear to have reported on the Puerto Rican municipalities' unprecedented RICO lawsuit against Chevron, ExxonMobil, Shell, and other Big Oil companies. Among independent news outlets, Grist, the *Guardian*, and the *American Prospect* published stories of their own after the initial reports by Common Dreams and Reuters.[77]

Leaks Reveal Homeland Security Plans to Regulate Disinformation Online

Ken Klippenstein and Lee Fang, "Truth Cops: Leaked Documents Outline DHS's Plans to Police Disinformation," The Intercept, October 31, 2022.

Student Researcher: Reagan Haynie (Loyola Marymount University)

Faculty Evaluator: Mickey Huff (Diablo Valley College)

A series of leaks have exposed plans by the Department of Homeland Security (DHS) to ramp up censorship of dangerous speech online. According to an October 2022 report from the Intercept, DHS announced a new "Disinformation Governance Board" in early 2022.[78] The board's goals were to police "misinformation (false information spread unintentionally), disinformation (false information spread intentionally), and malinformation (factual information shared, typically out of context, with harmful intent) that allegedly threatens U.S. interests," the Intercept's Ken Klippenstein and Lee Fang explained.

Records seized in a lawsuit filed by Missouri's attorney general, Eric Schmitt, show how the US government uses its power and influence to shape discourse online. Leaked records from the Cybersecurity and Infrastructure Agency's (CISA) Cybersecurity Advisory Committee contain various discussions concerning the range and limits of US influence over online discourse and conversations surrounding strategies to successfully remove false or intentionally misleading information from social media platforms.

The Intercept cited another CISA document, in which FBI official Laura Dehmlow claimed that support for the US government could be undermined by subversive social media content. The meeting where Dehmlow discussed this matter was attended by multiple Twitter executives and senior executives from JPMorgan Chase.

When the Intercept asked about Twitter's participation, a company spokesperson wrote, "We do not coordinate with other entities when making content moderation decisions, and we independently evaluate content in line with the Twitter Rules." Facebook and Instagram, however, have different policies and regulations for government officials. These sites include dedicated "portals" that allow government officials to directly flag and suppress information they deem unfit under government policy regulations.

Efforts to combat misinformation online increased following a series of high-profile hacking incidents at US firms in 2018. The Cybersecurity and Infrastructure Security Agency Act was signed and enacted in response. This law created a new section of the DHS committed to policing disinformation. Under this policy, it is standard protocol for state officials to send examples of disinformation to CISA, which then forwards them to the tech companies for their response.

According to the Intercept, despite eventually disbanding its Disinformation Governance Board, DHS intends to expand its efforts at policing online content to target "inaccurate information on the origins of the COVID-19 pandemic, the efficacy of COVID-19 vaccines, racial justice, the U.S. withdrawal from Afghanistan, and the nature of U.S. support to Ukraine."

The Intercept's reporting was referenced by the *Washington Post* in its coverage of the DHS leaks.[79] However, the *Post* did not mention DHS's plans to target misinformation concerning COVID-19 vaccines, racial injustice, the US withdrawal from Afghanistan, or US support of Ukraine. The *Post*'s reporting also failed to mention the Facebook portal that allows DHS and government partners to report disinformation directly to the company. Fox News twice referenced the Intercept report, though its coverage focused mostly on politicians' reactions to the leaks.[80] ABC News, citing the same Intercept report, published a short web post examining the DHS's relationship with Facebook.[81] Conservative media outlets, including the *National Review* and *American Conservative*, also published articles examining DHS plans to target disinformation online that cited the Intercept's reporting on the subject.[82]

Debt Crisis Looms for World's Poorest Nations

Kaamil Ahmed, "World's Poorest Nations Spend 16% of Revenue on Debt, the Highest in 25 Years," *The Guardian*, April 11, 2023.

Phillip Inman, "World's Poorest Countries' Debt Interest Payments Rise 35%, Report Says," *The Guardian*, December 6, 2022.

Brett Wilkins, "1 in 3 of World's Poorest Countries Spend More on Debt Repayments Than Education," Common Dreams, October 11, 2022.

Student Researcher: Cem İsmail Addemir (Illinois State University)

Faculty Evaluator: Steve Macek (North Central College)

The world's poorest countries will pay 35 percent more in debt interest bills in 2023 than they did in 2022 due to costs associated with the COVID-19 pandemic and a dramatic increase in the price of imported food, as reported by the World Bank.[83] Seventy-five impoverished nations, most in sub-Saharan Africa, will spend roughly $62 billion to meet the repayment requirements of loans primarily obtained in the past decade, according to a December 2022 article from the *Guardian* by Phillip Inman. A *Guardian* article by Kaamil Ahmed, published in April 2023, reported that ninety-one low-income countries will spend more than 16 percent of their revenues on external debt repayments, the highest level in twenty-five years.

Poor countries are facing mounting difficulties repaying their debts due to soaring interest rates and the rise in the dollar's value since 2019, severely limiting their ability to finance their debts. Moreover, the World Bank expressed concern that debt payments by these countries consume funds needed for vital social services such as education and health care.

As Brett Wilkins reported in October 2022 for Common Dreams, a recent study by the UK-based charity Save the Children found that in 2020, a third of all low- and middle-income countries spent more on external debt repayment than education.[84] In a plea to rich countries, World Bank president David Malpass warned that forcing poor nations to divert cash from welfare programs to debt interest payments would likely produce "social unrest," Inman reported for the *Guardian*.

Developing countries have taken on increased debt over the last few years to cover healthcare spending during the pandemic and the growing costs of gas and food, Inman explained. Poor nations continue to lack the ability to offset these rising costs through increased taxes, forcing them to rely on loans from private lenders. By the end of 2021, Inman wrote, "61% of long-term public and publicly guaranteed debt worth $3.6tn was owed to private creditors rather than [governments of wealthy nations] or other official creditors, compared with 46% in 2010." Inman explained that the payback time for loans taken by developing countries from private financial institutions is typically less than half that of loans provided by wealthy governments, and the interest rates charged by private lenders are generally higher. At the same time, Inman observed that China and, to a lesser extent, India, Turkey, and Russia, have become major creditors for poor countries.

The elite financial media, including the *Wall Street Journal*, Bloomberg, CNBC, and the *Economist*, have heavily covered the looming debt crisis as an investment story, emphasizing the risk of default by African nations such as Ghana and Zambia.[85] Although reports by these financial news outlets have sometimes touched on the enormous humanitarian costs that surging debt-service payments impose on developing nations, typically the main concern of their reporting is financial stability rather than the evisceration of poor nations' educational and health systems and its consequences. Moreover, these outlets—and establishment newspapers such as the *Washington Post* and *New York Times*—have often framed their coverage in terms of demands by the US and other Western nations that China should offer debt relief to distressed debtor nations.[86] In the process, corporate coverage has obscured the key role of private creditors in squeezing ever-larger debt repayments from the world's poorest nations. The most popular commercial news media in the United States—including ABC, CBS, NBC, Fox News, and CNN—have largely ignored this story.

Economic Consequences of US Gun Violence "Far Costlier" Than Previously Known

Eric Westervelt, "American Gun Violence Has Immense Costs Beyond the Death Toll, New Studies Find," NPR, July 21, 2022.

Student Researcher: Lauren Reduzzi (Drew University)

Faculty Evaluator: Mickey Huff (Diablo Valley College)

Gun violence costs Americans an astounding $557 billion per year in direct, indirect, and long-term costs, according to a July 2022 study by gun-control advocacy group Everytown for Gun Safety, reported on by NPR. Everytown's study, "The Economic Cost of Gun Violence," firmly stated, "America cannot afford gun violence."[87]

As NPR journalist Eric Westervelt detailed in his report, the $557 billion figure—roughly 2.6 percent of the US gross domestic product—includes the "immediate costs of a shooting, such as the police response, investigations and ambulance services all the way to the long-term health care costs. The analysis also includes estimates for [victims'] lost earnings, costs incurred by the criminal justice system, the price of mental health care and more."

According to Westervelt, separate research published in the *Annals of Internal Medicine* documented a four-fold rise in healthcare spending from 2008 through 2018 related to non-fatal injuries caused by guns.[88] Together, Westervelt said, the two studies "underscore that the repercussions from firearm deaths and injuries are deeper, wider and far costlier than previously known."

The number of mass shootings in the United States has grown considerably in the past few years. In July 2022, the Gun Violence Archive, a nonprofit that tracks shootings in the United States, reported at least 314 mass shootings in 2022 alone and more than twenty-two thousand individuals whose lives were cut short by gun violence.[89]

The enormous economic costs of gun violence impact all Americans. According to the Everytown study, taxpayers, survivors, families, and employers pay an average of $7.79 million daily in health care costs.[90] American taxpayers pay more than $30 million every day in police and criminal justice costs for investigation, prosecution, and incarceration. And employers lose an average of $1.47 million daily in productivity, revenue, and costs required to recruit and train replacements for victims of gun violence. Overall, US society loses $1.34 billion daily in quality-of-life costs from the impacts of gun violence on shooting victims and their families. The annual cost for each resident in the country is about $1,698. However, states with weaker gun laws and more gun-related injuries and fatalities suffer more economically, with per capita costs for firearms violence double or more than in states with stronger gun restrictions.

In addition to NPR, *Time* also reported the estimated $557 billion total annual cost of gun violence in the United States. The *Time* article referenced a special issue of the medical journal *JAMA* on gun violence, which cited the Everytown study as its source for the statistic.[91] Other corporate news outlets have sometimes covered the economic costs of gun violence but without citing the July 2022 Everytown study or its estimate of the astronomically high total cost of firearm violence.[92]

Derailment Furor Ignores Alarming Frequency of Toxic Chemical Spills

Carey Gillam, "Revealed: The US is Averaging One Chemical Accident Every Two Days," *The Guardian*, February 25, 2023.

Student Researcher: Julia Broberg (Frostburg State University)

Faculty Evaluator: Andy Duncan (Frostburg State University)

After a Norfolk Southern train filled with hazardous chemicals derailed outside the town of East Palestine, Ohio, on February 3, 2023, causing a toxic inferno and a mass evacuation, corporate news media provided around-the-clock coverage. TV correspondents dutifully interviewed displaced residents, attended press briefings about the disaster, and interviewed irate politicians, such as Ohio governor Mike DeWine and others. Yet for all the attention TV networks such as CNN and Fox focused on the accident and the thousands of gallons of toxic vinyl chloride it released, establishment media failed to report adequately on the frequency with which such chemical spills occur and the danger that routine chemical releases pose to millions of Americans.

Citing research by the Coalition to Prevent Chemical Disasters, Carey Gillam reported for the *Guardian* that 470 toxic chemical releases occurred in the United States between April 2020 and February 2023, roughly one incident every two days.[93] Although the incidents the CPCD tallied varied in severity, in each case they involved "the accidental release of chemicals deemed to pose potential threats to human and environmental health."

One example detailed in Gillam's article was a September 2022 spill of caustic substances at a recycling plant in California, which sent nine people to the hospital and prompted the evacuation of hundreds more. Another example cited was the rupture in December 2022 of a pipeline in northern Kansas that flooded the surrounding area with "588,000 gallons of diluted bitumen crude oil." Hundreds of workers are still trying to mitigate the impacts of that accident.

Although ten of the spills during the past two years

identified by CPCD involved rail accidents, most toxic chemical releases occur at facilities where chemicals are manufactured and stored. The Government Accountability Office has estimated there are twelve thousand such facilities in the United States and that roughly two hundred million people are at "regular risk" of accidental exposure to dangerous chemicals.[94] Many of those at greatest risk are "people of color, or otherwise disadvantaged communities," Gillam reported.

Environmental Protection Agency (EPA) data reveals there were roughly 160 accidents per year at chemical manufacturing and storage facilities between 2004 and 2013 and that the severity of accidental chemical releases is only getting worse. The EPA pushed for regulatory changes designed to enhance the safety of those living near chemical processing and storage faculties. However, Gillam reported, big business lobbyists such as the US Chamber of Commerce, the American Chemistry Council, and the American Petroleum Institute have "pushed back against stronger regulations."

Other independent news outlets have covered the increasing frequency of toxic chemical spills. For instance, in March 2023, the environmental news site Grist covered a toxic spill at a factory near Philadelphia, noting that the accident was one of fifty such incidents in the first three months of 2023, according to Coalition to Prevent Chemical Disasters figures.[95] However, despite the media frenzy surrounding the East Palestine derailment, as of May 2023, there has been *zero* corporate news coverage of the alarming number of accidental toxic chemical releases tracked by the CPCD. For a critical analysis of how establishment media covered the East Palestine derailment disaster, see chapter 4 of this volume, on News Abuse, by Robin Andersen.

Nearly Half of Unhoused People Are Employed

Julia Pagaduan, "Employed and Experiencing Homelessness: What the Numbers Show," National Alliance to End Homelessness, September 2, 2022.

Student Researcher: Annie Koruga (Ohlone College)

Faculty Evaluator: Robin Takahashi (Ohlone College)

Contrary to popular belief, many people who experience homelessness are employed, Julia Pagaduan reported for the National Alliance to End Homelessness in September 2022. Drawing on a study produced by the Becker Friedman Institute for Economics at the University of Chicago, Pagaduan reported that 53 percent of the sheltered unhoused population and 40 percent of the unsheltered unhoused population were employed either part- or full-time from 2011 to 2018.[96]

Unhoused people in shelters earned more than those who were unsheltered. In 2015, the mean pre-tax income for the former group was $8,169, while the mean income for the latter was $6,934. According to the National Low Income Housing Coalition, one would need to make approximately $21.25 per hour to afford a one-bedroom apartment.[97] "Even if people are working full time, they would not be able to afford housing earning minimum wage," Pagaduan reported.

Several barriers hinder unhoused people's ability to gain and maintain employment, Pagaduan explained. Job applicants may face obstacles such as employers requiring a permanent address, logistical hurdles for transportation and personal hygiene, needing accommodations for disabilities, and general hiring challenges, including educational requirements. Furthermore, unhoused people may lose access to vital social services if they exceed low-income thresholds.

Even when unhoused individuals can afford rent, Pagaduan noted, "landlord discrimination against past or current homelessness, eviction history, involvement of criminal justice, and income source can all prevent people from achieving housing security. Barriers like these can keep people homeless—even if they're working, and even if there are affordable units available in their area."

Although corporate news media have occasionally noted the problem, coverage has tended to focus on the plight of individuals or the low wages of particular sectors. In May 2023, for example, the *Los Angeles Times* and CBS News cited an Economic Roundtable study that found "fast-food workers represent 1 in 17 of homeless people in California."[98] The *Los Angeles Times* also reported on a RAND study that found "front line workers essential to solving Los Angeles County's homelessness crisis do not make enough money to afford housing themselves."[99] No corporate outlets have shed light on the scale and scope of the problem presented by the National Coalition to End Homelessness.

Public Health Threatened by Beef Suppliers' Continued Use of "Critically Important" Antibiotics

Ben Stockton and Andrew Wasley, "McDonald's and Walmart Beef Suppliers Risk Public Health With 'Reckless' Antibiotic Use," Bureau of Investigative Journalism, and, "McDonald's and Walmart Beef Suppliers Criticized for 'Reckless' Antibiotics Use," *The Guardian*, November 21, 2022.

Student Researcher: Hailey Hearney (Drew University)

Faculty Researcher: Lisa Lynch (Drew University)

Beef suppliers for major fast food and supermarket chains are sourcing meat from US farms that use antibiotics linked to the spread of "superbugs," bacteria strains that are resistant to antibiotics, the Bureau of Investigative Journalism and the *Guardian* reported in November 2022. The joint investigation examined US Department of Agriculture data from 2017-2022 for ten of the biggest meat packers—including Cargill, JBS, and Green Bay Dressed Beef—and found that all ten sourced beef from farms that use at least one antibiotic designated "highest priority" and "critically important." Cattle farms selling to JBS, which has supplied beef to Wendy's, Walmart, and Taco Bell, and to Green Bay Dressed Beef, a supplier for the Kroger supermarket chain, have used as many as seven highest priority critically important antibiotics (or HP-CIAs). Drugs designated as HP-CIAs are often the "last line" of treatment available for serious bacterial infections in humans.

The spread of drug-resistant bacteria "represents a huge public health challenge," the *Guardian* and the Bureau of Investigative Journalism (TBIJ) reported.[100] The World Health Organization has warned that antibiotics essential to human medicine should not be used in livestock because bacteria can develop resistance that reduces the drugs' effectiveness for humans. According to the Centers for Disease Control and Prevention, antibiotic resistance causes more than thirty-five thousand deaths in the United States each year and 1.3 million deaths globally.

Since 2017, the United States has banned the use of antibiotics to promote livestock growth, but cattle farmers can still obtain veterinary prescriptions for antibiotics to prevent or treat disease.

McDonald's has "repeatedly dodged calls for it to set targets to reduce the use of antibiotics by farmers supplying it with beef," the *Guardian* and TBIJ reported. Matt Wellington of the US Public Interest Research Group described McDonald's failure to commit to reductions as "a major blow," noting that it "sets a bad example for the rest of the industry."

As of May 2023, no major corporate news outlets have covered the findings of the joint TBIJ-*Guardian* investigation. Shortly after that study's publication, the *New York Times* website posted a transcript of an episode of "The Ezra Klein Show" that featured Leah Garcés, president of the international nonprofit Mercy for Animals, discussing "The Hidden Costs of Cheap Meat," including the threats to human health posed by antibiotic resistance.[101] Subsequent coverage of the Bureau and the *Guardian*'s study has been limited to other independent news sources, including the health website Eat This,

Not That!; *Deseret News*; *Corporate Wellness Magazine*; and *Scientific American*.[102]

"Informal Removal" Policies Deny Educational Opportunities for Students With Disabilities

Meredith Kolodner and Annie Ma, "When Your Disability Gets You Sent Home from School," The Hechinger Report; and "Kids With Disabilities Face Off-The-Books School Suspensions," Associated Press, October 4, 2022.

Student Researchers: Isabella Arbelaez, Taylor Callahan, Alexa DeMaria, and Talia Panacy (University of Massachusetts Amherst)

Faculty Evaluator: Allison Butler (University of Massachusetts Amherst)

Across the United States, students with disabilities are being sent home from school because of behavioral issues in the classroom. In an October 2022 article for the Hechinger Report and the Associated Press, Meredith Kolodner and Annie Ma reported that, under a policy of "informal removal," students across the country are being sent home from school because of behavioral issues that stem from their disabilities, but this missed class time is neither counted as suspension nor documented by school administrations.

Kolodner and Ma explained that informal removal is defined by the Department of Education as "an action taken by school staff in response to a child's behavior that excludes the child for part or all of the school day—or even indefinitely." Excessive use of informal removals, they reported, "amounts to a form of off-the-books discipline—a de facto denial of education that evades accountability."

Due to the nationwide shortage of teachers, students with behavioral needs are often pushed out of the classroom because inadequately trained teachers cannot handle the disruptions. Students of color with disabilities are disproportionately affected, even though federal law prohibits students from being disciplined or barred from class for behavior related to their disabilities.

The COVID-19 pandemic has exacerbated the frequency and consequences of "informal removal." According to Catherine E. Lhamon, assistant secretary for the Department of Education's Office for Civil Rights, "The practice has taken hold in a way that is dangerous for students and needs to be addressed."

This issue affects not only students but also their parents. The Associated Press and the Hechinger Report interviewed twenty families in ten states with children who had been subjected to informal removal. Some parents reported having lost jobs because they had to leave work so frequently to pick up children who had been removed from classrooms; other parents said they had to choose new schools or even districts because of removal policies.

Despite the story's significance and the Hechinger Report's partnership with the Associated Press—a news service from which many other prominent news organizations source stories—the issue of informal removals of students with disabilities has received meager coverage from most establishment news outlets. When treated as news, the issue has typically been reported as a local story.[103] Though important, locally-focused coverage cannot convey the national scope of the problem. One exception to this pattern was an in-depth article by Erica L. Green for the *New York Times* that described informal removals as "pernicious practices that harm some of the nation's most vulnerable children."[104]

Twitter Files Reveal US Government Pressure on Social Media Platform to Suppress Alternative Views

Matt Taibbi, "Capsule Summaries of All Twitter Files Threads to Date, With Links and a Glossary," Racket News, January 4, 2023.

Matt Taibbi, "My Statement to Congress," Racket News, March 9, 2023.

Kenan Malik, "The Twitter Files Should Disturb Liberal Critics of Elon Musk—and Here's Why," *The Guardian,* January 1, 2023.

Student Researcher: Kruthi Battar (San Francisco State University)

Faculty Evaluator: Kenn Burrows (San Francisco State University)

The "Twitter Files"—a trove of internal communications relating to Twitter's content moderation practices, made available to select journalists by the platform's owner, Elon Musk—reveal how pressure from US government agencies has shaped political content on the popular social networking service.

Twitter has banned selected political voices, supported covert government operations, censored posts exploding the myth of large-scale Russian interference in the 2016 election, silenced anti-vaccine activists, and more. The following examples of the released files, as presented by journalist Matt Taibbi at Racket News, suggest the extent of government intrusion into Twitter's operations:

▣ Secret Blacklists (Twitter Files Parts 2, 3, and 4): Twitter has a large toolbox for controlling the visibility of any user. The platform aggressively applied "visibility filtering" to the account of Donald Trump before eventually banning him altogether after his supporters stormed the US Capitol on January 6, 2021.

▣ Assistance to the Pentagon for Covert Online Psyops (Twitter Files Part 8): Twitter officials testified publicly to Congress that the company did not allow government-backed covert operations, even while it was a clear partner in state-backed programs involving fake accounts. For example, the US Central Command (CENTCOM) maintained fifty-two Arab-language accounts on Twitter "to amplify certain messages."

▣ Congressional Requests for Bans (Twitter Files Part 14): Former head of the House Intelligence Committee Adam Schiff (D-CA) and Democratic National Committee colleagues not only "asked for the takedown of an obvious satire" of President Biden, Taibbi reported, but also "requested takedowns of accounts that were critical of the Steele dossier and outed the name of the supposed 'whistleblower' in the Ukrainegate case, Eric Ciaramella." Schiff's staffers reportedly thanked Twitter for its efforts to "de-amplify" certain accounts.

◉ Flagging and Removing Accurate Information (Twitter Files Part 19): In March 2023, via Taibbi's Twitter Files release, researcher Andrew Lowenthal disclosed how four think tanks and multiple government agencies worked to create a cross-platform system for seven major internet platforms—including Twitter, Instagram, and TikTok—to aid in identifying and labeling "disinformation events." The system was used to flag verifiably true stories online about COVID-19 vaccine side effects to be deleted or "de-amplified."

Unfortunately, as Kenan Malik pointed out in a January 2023 report for the *Guardian*, despite giving Taibbi and a few other handpicked journalists exclusive access to the Twitter files, Musk has resisted calls to provide additional journalists and academic researchers broader access to Twitter's internal records of its content moderation decisions. As Malik wrote, "Musk seems more interested in being seen to 'own the libs' than in opening up Twitter's inner workings."

Establishment news media have failed to explore the full implications of the Twitter Files coverage by Taibbi, Malik, and others. For example, NPR claimed, "Elon

Musk is using the Twitter Files to discredit foes and push conspiracy theories"; *The Atlantic* called the Twitter Files "sloppy, anecdotal, devoid of context, and, well, old news," while CBS News downplayed the files' importance, presenting Twitter as a company doing the best it could and government involvement as minimal.[105]

Activism Targets Outdated State Laws That Criminalize HIV

Adam M. Rhodes, "Pressure Mounts against HIV Criminalization as Prosecutions Continue," The Appeal, September 15, 2022.

Amelia Abraham, "'I Lost My Retirement, My Career, My Home': The Americans Imprisoned for Being HIV-Positive," *The Guardian*, December 1, 2022.

Victoria Law, "People with HIV Are Still Being Criminalized in 25 States," Truthout, January 25, 2023.

Student Researchers: Jessica Jean-Baptiste (SUNY Cortland) and Joey Douille (Loyola Marymount University)

Faculty Evaluators: Christina Knopf (SUNY Cortland) and Kyra Pearson (Loyola Marymount University)

Laws that criminalize HIV transmission—many enacted in the 1980s, when HIV was poorly understood—have not been changed to reflect scientific advances in the treatment of HIV/AIDS. In January 2023, Truthout reported that twenty-five states have HIV-specific laws, and nine states have sentence enhancements that apply to HIV+ people. Black men and women and White women are disproportionately affected by these outdated statutes, according to UCLA's Williams Institute, which studies sexual orientation, gender identity, and public policy.[106]

The overall number of people arrested under HIV criminalization laws in the United States is not officially tracked, according to the *Guardian*, but the HIV Justice Network had counted 2,936 such cases at the time of the *Guardian's* report, a figure that likely underestimated the actual number of arrests. As Truthout and The Appeal reported, not all states require transmission of the virus or intent to transmit it for convictions.

Existing HIV laws are at odds with current scientific understanding and medical treatment of HIV. For example, eight states criminalize the act of exposing another person to HIV through spitting, even though saliva does not transmit HIV.[107] One group seeking legal reform of outdated HIV laws is the Elizabeth Taylor AIDS Foundation. The Foundation's "HIV Is Not a Crime" campaign aims to bring laws "up to date with contemporary science," including what is known as "U=U," meaning that HIV that is undetectable due to therapeutic medication is untransmittable. According to Catherine Brown, the foundation's executive director, the laws that remain on the books are a result of HIV stigma, because other viruses are not criminalized in the same way.

Kerry Thomas, who is serving a thirty-year sentence in an Idaho prison for not disclosing his HIV status to his then-partner, told Truthout, "Criminalization is not prevention. Treatment is prevention." Many activists hope to see HIV criminalization laws completely abolished. One possible avenue toward this goal was proposed in a 2021 *Yale Law Journal* article by Joshua Blecher-Cohen, who argued that HIV criminalization laws violate the Americans with Disabilities Act, which "explicitly applies to people living with HIV or AIDs," The Appeal reported.

The establishment press rarely covers laws that criminalize HIV non-disclosure, exposure, or transmission—or organized campaigns to reform those laws. In a December 2021 article on HIV-related arrests in Kentucky, NBC News did so, citing a report from the Williams Institute, but NBC's report selectively focused on the impacts of Kentucky's HIV laws on women and sex workers, even though the Williams Institute's report also highlighted significant differences in the rates at which Black men and women were arrested, compared to White men and women.[108] In November 2022, the Biden-Harris administration announced several initiatives intended to "advance equity and opportunity," including a "National HIV/AIDS Strategy" that, according to a White House briefing, will encourage "reform of state HIV criminalization laws" as one step toward "ending the HIV epidemic in the United States by 2030."[109]

HONORABLE MENTIONS

New College Textbooks Include Less About Climate Change

Caroline Preston, "Coverage of Climate Change in College Textbooks Is Headed in The Wrong Direction," The Hechinger Report, December 21, 2022.

North Carolina State University researchers have found that current editions of college textbooks provide less coverage of the climate crisis than previous editions did. According to the study of fifty-seven college biology textbooks published between 1970 and 2019, "The number of research publications between 1970 and 2019 has grown exponentially, but the proportion of textbook coverage has decreased from one textbook sentence per 200 scientific publications to one textbook sentence per 1,100 scientific publications."

Biden Administration "Gag Order" Censors Federal Scientists

Tom Perkins, "Biden Administration's Rule for Federal Scientists Is a 'Gag Order', Critics Say," *The Guardian*, February 10, 2023.

Julia Conley, "Experts Condemn Biden Admin's Proposed 'Gag Rule' for Federal Scientists," Common Dreams, February 10, 2023.

In January 2023, the Biden administration implemented a rule that restrains federal scientists from addressing controversial research topics to the public, the *Guardian* reported in February 2023. The White House Office of Science and Technology Policy unveiled a rule requiring scientists to receive approval before publishing opinions and research on topics connected to government policy. Climate change, chemical contamination, and biosafety are among the controversial issues impacted by the order.

New Privacy Law Thwarts Reporting on Judicial Conflicts of Interest

Seth Stern, "Judges Can Now Censor the Internet on the Taxpayer Dime," Freedom of the Press Foundation, January 12, 2023.

In December 2022, President Biden signed a bill into law that allows federal judges to order the redaction of their and their relatives' "covered information" (such as home addresses, schools, and employers) from public records, to protect them from harassment. The Daniel Anderl Judicial Security and Privacy Act has already allowed more than one thousand judges to order the removal of personal information on the internet, making it harder for reporters to expose conflicts of interest involving federal judges and their families.

Bogus Copyright Complaints Throttle Investigative Journalism

"Fake Copyright Complaints Seek to Remove Reports on Minister and Lawyer," Organized Crime and Corruption Reporting Project, March 1, 2023.

BBC Trending, "How Fake Copyright Complaints Are Muzzling Journalists," BBC, March 2, 2023.

News reports critical of powerful oil lobbyists in Equatorial Guinea have been subject to takedown following bogus copyright claims. Anonymous individuals create copies of the articles they seek to censor, with fake publication dates preexisting those of the original articles. These individuals then issue a copyright infringement claim under the US Digital Millennium Copyright Act (DMCA) to the servers that host the original articles. The process differs depending on the server, but the bogus complaints can keep content blocked for weeks while the original author proves their credentials. "These bogus allegations look like a devious tactic to suppress independent journalism," according to the editor of one of the affected news outlets, Megan Darby of Climate Home News.

Title IX Invoked to Stifle Campus Journalism

Lindsie Rank, "Title IX Weaponized Against Student Journalists, Again. This Time, at Princeton," FIRE (Foundation for Individual Rights and Expression), September 28, 2022.

Title IX—the landmark civil rights law that prohibits sex-based discrimination in any school or any other education program that receives funding from the federal government—is being invoked to constrain campus journalism and student journalists. As Lindsie Rank reported for FIRE, colleges and universities are required, ethically and legally, to do their part to prevent sexual discrimination on campus, but "nothing in the language of Title IX or its attendant guidelines requires institutions to silence journalists, either through no-contact orders or overbroad mandatory reporting policies."

LIBBY MEAGHER is a senior Communication Studies major at North Central College. A new member of the Project Censored team, she worked as a student research assistant, fact-checking, editing, and rewriting stories for this year's book.

GRACE HARTY is a senior majoring in Communication Studies and minoring in Writing at North Central College. She plans on following her dreams as a writer after she graduates.

AMY GRIM BUXBAUM is an Associate Professor of Communication at North Central College in Naperville, IL, where she teaches courses in organizational communication and rhetoric.

STEVE MACEK is a Professor of Communication and Media Studies at North Central College and serves as co-coordinator of Project Censored's campus affiliate program. He writes frequently about censorship and First Amendment issues for Truthout, Common Dreams, and other independent media outlets.

ANDY LEE ROTH is associate director of Project Censored. A coauthor of *The Media and Me*, the Project's guide to critical media literacy, he has also written for *Index on Censorship*, *YES! Magazine*, Truthout, *In These Times*, and the *International Journal of Press/Politics*.

Notes

1 On framing and critical media literacy, see Project Censored and the Media Revolution Collective, *The Media and Me: A Guide to Critical Media Literacy for Young People* (Fair Oaks, CA and New York: The Censored Press and Seven Stories Press, 2022).

2 Walter Lippmann, *Liberty and the News* (Princeton: Princeton University Press, 2008 [1920]), 9. Lippmann examined news, propaganda, and censorship as crucial factors in what he first described in this book as "the manufacture of consent" (pp. 2, 37) an original formulation that has since exerted a profound influence on nearly every critical study of news and politics.

3 For information on how to nominate a story, see "How to Support Project Censored" at the back of this volume.

4 Validated Independent News stories are archived on the Project Censored website.

5 For a complete list of the Project's judges and their brief biographies, see the acknowledgments at the back of this volume.

6 Ian T. Cousins et al., "Outside the Safe Operating Space of a New Planetary Boundary for Per- and Polyfluoroalkyl Substances (PFAS)," *Environmental Science & Technology* 56, no. 16 (August 2, 2022): 11172-79.

7 "It's Raining PFAS: Even in Antarctica and on the Tibetan Plateau Rainwater Is Unsafe to Drink," Stockholm University, August 19, 2022.

8 Viken Kantarci, "Rainwater Unsafe to Drink Due to Chemicals: Study," ABS-CBN News, August 10, 2022.

9 "Our Current Understanding of the Human Health and Environmental Risks of PFAS," United States Environmental Protection Agency, updated June 7, 2023.

10 EPA Press Office, "EPA Announces New Drinking Water Health Advisories for PFAS Chemicals, $1 Billion in Bipartisan Infrastructure Law Funding to Strengthen Health Protections," United States Environmental Protection Agency, June 15, 2022.

11 Dino Grandoni, "EPA Finally Move to Label Some 'Forever Chemicals' as Hazardous," *Washington Post*, August 26, 2022.

12 Isabella Grullón Paz, "PFAS: The 'Forever Chemicals' You Couldn't Escape if You Tried," *New York Times*, April 12, 2022, updated June 3, 2023.

13 Wyatte Grantham-Philips, "Rainwater Is Now Unsafe to Drink Worldwide Because of 'Forever Chemicals,' Study Suggests," *USA Today*, August 13, 2022; Chloe Dionisio, "All Rainwater Is Unsafe to Drink According to Study," Discovery, August 15, 2022; Corrie Pelc, "PFAS in Rainwater: What It Means for Health," Medical News Today, August 3, 2022.

14 Kris Maher and Bob Tita, "3M to Stop Making, Discontinue Use of 'Forever Chemicals'," *Wall Street Journal*, December 20, 2022.

15 Seema Mody, "States Sue 3M, Dupont Over Toxic 'Forever Chemicals' Found in Drinking Water," CNBC, June 2, 2023.

16 John Flesher, "$1.18 Billion Deal Reached Over Drinking Water Contamination by 'Forever Chemicals'," *PBS NewsHour*, June 5, 2023.

17 Nadia Gaber, Lisa Bero, and Tracey J. Woodruff, "The Devil They Knew: Chemical Documents Analysis of Industry Influence on PFAS Science," *Annals of Global Health* 89, no. 1 (2023).

18 Witness to War, "Former CIA Agent John Stockwell Talks about How the CIA Worked in Vietnam and Elsewhere," YouTube, September 29, 2017, video, 15:12.

19 Danielle Abril, "Powering the Picket Line: Workers Are Turning to Tech in Their Labor," *Washington Post*, October 18, 2021.

20 See, e.g., Mark Mazzetti, Ronen Bergman, and Matina Stevis-Gridneff, "How the Global Spyware Industry Spiraled Out of Control," *New York Times*, December 8, 2022, updated January 28, 2023; and Christopher Mims, "The Russia-Ukraine Cyberwar Could Outlast the Shooting War," *Wall Street Journal*, March 5, 2022.

21 Alfredo Carpineti, "'Forever Chemicals' Makers Covered Up Health Risks for Decades, Secret Documents Reveal," IFLScience, June 1, 2023; Nadia Gaber, Lisa Bero, and Tracey J. Woodruff, "The Devil They Knew: Chemical Documents Analysis of Industry Influence on PFAS Science," *Annals of Global Health* 89, no. 1 (June 1, 2023).

22 Tod Hardin, "PFAS Are Costing Society Over $17 Trillion per Year Worldwide," DCReport, May 13, 2023.

23 Dino Grandoni, "EPA Finally Moves to Label Some 'Forever Chemicals' as Hazardous," *Washington Post*, August 26, 2022; Timothy Puko, "EPA Struggles to Ban Asbestos, Other Chemicals Years After Congress Granted New Powers," *Washington Post*, February 19, 2023; Lisa Friedman, "Biden Administration to Restrict Cancer-Causing 'Forever Chemicals'," *New York Times*, March 14, 2023, updated June 22, 2023; Eric Lipton, "Public Health vs. Economic Growth: Toxic Chemical Rules Pose Test for Biden," *New York Times*, March 16, 2023.

24 "A Glimpse From the Field: How Abusers Are Misusing Technology," Safety Net Project (National Network to End Domestic Violence), February 17, 2015; Jason Koebler, "'I See You': A Domestic Violence Survivor Talks About Being Surveilled by Her Ex," Vice, March 17, 2017.

25 Albert Fox Cahn, "The Most Devastating Tool of Abortion Bounty Hunters in Texas Could Be the Surveillance State," *Fast Company*, September 14, 2021.

26 Emma Woollacott, "What Does the Recent Abortion Ruling Mean for US Privacy Legislation?" Cybernews, July 4, 2022.

27 Eric D. Perakslis, Katie D. McMillan and Jessilyn Dunn, "Proposed Rules to Protect Health Data in an Era of Abortion Bans Fall Short," STAT, May 12, 2023.

28 Geoffrey A. Fowler and Tatum Hunter, "For People Seeking Abortions, Digital Privacy Is Suddenly Critical," *Washington Post*, May 4, 2022, updated June 24, 2022; Cynthia Conti-Cook and Kate Bertash, "Op-Ed:

The End of Roe Means We'll Be Criminalized for More of Our Data,"
Los Angeles Times, May 16, 2022; Natasha Singer and Brian X. Chen, "In
a Post-Roe World, the Future of Digital Privacy Looks Even Grimmer,"
New York Times, July 13, 2022, updated July 20, 2022; "How US Police Use
Digital Data to Prosecute Abortions," *Financial Press*, January 28, 2023.

29   Alejandro Guizar-Coutiño et al., "A Global Evaluation of the Effec-
tiveness of Voluntary REDD+ Projects at Reducing Deforestation and
Degradation in the Moist Tropics," *Conservation Biology* (Society for
Conservation Biology) 36, no. 6 (December 2022).

30   "Verra Response to Guardian Article on Carbon Offsets," Verra, January
18, 2023.

31   "Total's Congo Offsetting Project 'Snatched Our Land'," SourceMaterial,
December 12, 2022. We thank Santo Carroccia and Lisa Lynch of Drew
University for bringing this story to Project Censored's attention.

32   Patrick Greenfield, "Biggest Carbon Credit Certifier to Replace Its
Rainforest Offsets Scheme," *The Guardian*, March 10, 2023.

33   Shane Shifflett, "Companies Are Buying Large Numbers of Carbon
Offsets That Don't Cut Emissions," *Wall Street Journal*, September 8, 2022.

34   Taylor Moore, "Here's How Carbon Offsets Can Live Up to Their Bold
Promises," *Time*, October 28, 2022.

35   The Editorial Board, "Are the Liberal Elites Coming for Your Gas Stove?"
Chicago Tribune, January 19, 2023. On the panic, promoted by Republican
lawmakers, see, e.g., Nikki McCann Ramirez, "No, the Government Is
Not Seizing Your Gas Stove," *Rolling Stone*, January 11, 2023.

36   Office of Public Affairs, "Election Petitions Up 53%, Board Continues To
Reduce Case Processing Time in FY22," National Labor Relations Board,
October 6, 2022.

37   Justin McCarthy, "U.S. Approval of Labor Unions the Highest Since
1965," Gallup, August 30, 2022.

38   Marick Masters, "Worker Strikes and Union Elections Surged in 2022—
Could It Mark A Turning Point For Organized Labor?" Yahoo, January 5,
2023; Rani Molla, "How Unions Are Winning Again, In 4 Charts," Vox,
August 30, 2022; Ian Kullgren, "Rise of Organizing Spotlights Rules on
How Union Elections Work," Bloomberg Law, August 29, 2022; Lauren
Kaori Gurley, "The Labor Market Is Still Red Hot—And It's Helping
Labor Union Organizers," *Washington Post*, August 30, 2022.

39   Taylor Johnston, "The U.S. Labor Movement Is Popular, Prominent and
Also Shrinking," *New York Times*, January 25, 2022.

40   Lea Di Salvatore, "Investor-State Disputes in the Fossil Fuel Industry,"
International Institute for Sustainable Development, December 31, 2021.

41   Samuel Webb, "Fossil Fuel Firms Sue Governments for £13bn Over
Climate Action," Independent, September 17, 2021.

42   Mary D. Willis et al., "Associations Between Residential Proximity to Oil
and Gas Extraction and Hypertensive Conditions During Pregnancy: A
Difference-In-Differences Analysis in Texas, 1996–2009," *International
Journal of Epidemiology* 51, no. 2 (April 2022): 525-36.

43   On the impacts of fracking, see, e.g., "Compendium of Scientific, Medical, and Media Findings Demonstrating Risks and Harms of Fracking
and Associated Gas and Oil Infrastructure," Physicians for Social
Responsibility, April 28, 2022; and previous coverage by Project Censored,

including Rayne Madison et al., "Fracking Our Food Supply," story #18 and Lyndsey Casey and Peter Phillips, "Pennsylvania Law Gags Doctors to Protect Big Oil's 'Proprietary Secrets,'" story #22, from 2012–2013; and Carolina de Mello et al., "Oil Industry Illegally Dumps Fracking Wastewater," story #2 from 2014–2015, each of which is archived on the Project's website.

44   Cassandra J. Clark et al., "Unconventional Oil and Gas Development Exposure and Risk of Childhood Acute Lymphoblastic Leukemia: A Case–Control Study in Pennsylvania, 2009–2017," *Environmental Health Perspectives* 130, no. 8 (August 17, 2022).

45   Will Sullivan, "Children Living Near Fracking Sites Have an Increased Risk for Leukemia, Study Suggests," *Smithsonian*, August 25, 2022; Sharon Udasin, "Children Who Live Near Fracking Sites at Birth Face Increased Risk of Leukemia: Study," The Hill, August 17, 2021; Susan Phillips, "Children Living Near Pa. Fracking Sites Are at Increased Risk of Leukemia, Study Finds," WHYY (NPR), August 17, 2022.

46   Elliott Davis Jr., "The States Most Threatened by Oil and Gas Pollution," *U.S. News & World Report*, June 6, 2022.

47   Ali Hines, "Decade of Defiance," Global Witness, September 29, 2022, updated May 10, 2023.

48   Hines, "Decade of Defiance."

49   Emily Pontecorvo, "Land Defenders Face Violence and Repression. Clean Energy Could Make it Worse," Grist, April 6, 2022.

50   Oscar Lopez, "Mexico Named Deadliest Country for Environmental Activists," *New York Times*, September 29, 2022.

51   Manuela Andreoni, "Where Defending Nature Can Be Deadly," *New York Times*, October 4, 2022, updated May 22, 2023.

52   Rafael E. Lozano and Anjan Sundaram, "The Deadly Costs for Mexico's Indigenous Communities Fighting Climate Change," *Los Angeles Times,* February 26, 2023.

53   See Rachel Song, Inga Van Buren, and Andy Lee Roth, "Global Killing of Environmentalists Rises Drastically," story #22 from 2014–2015, accessible online in Project Censored's archive of its annual Top 25 story lists.

54   Elise Gould and Jori Kandra, "Inequality in Annual Earnings Worsens in 2021," Economic Policy Institute, December 21, 2022.

55   "Big Oil Boasts a Record-Setting $52 Billion in Quarterly Profits While Consumers Continue to Suffer Under High Gas Prices," Accountable. US, July 2022.

56   Sarah Anderson, "Wall Street Bonuses Soar By 20%, Nearly 5 Times the Increase in US Average Weekly Earnings," Inequality.org, March 23, 2022.

57   Wall Street bonuses fell by 26 percent in 2022, partly due to rising interest rates and growing recession fears; see, for example, Jeanne Sahadi, "The Average Wall Street Bonus Fell By 26% Last Year," CNN, March 30, 2023.

58   Reade Pickert, "US Corporate Profits Soar With Margins at Widest Since 1950," Bloomberg, August 25, 2022.

59   Max Zahn, "Are Record Corporate Profits Driving Inflation? Here's What Experts Think," ABC News, June 30, 2022.

60 Lydia DePillis, "Is 'Greedflation' Rewriting Economics, or Do Old Rules Still Apply?" *New York Times,* June 3, 2022.

61 Juliana Kaplan and Madison Hoff, "The Next Recession Might Hit The Wealthy More—And a 'Richcession' Could Be Good News for Low-Wage Workers," Insider, January 5, 2023.

62 Noor Zainab Hussain and Elizabeth Dilts Marshall, "Wall Street Hands Out Biggest Bonuses Since 2006," Reuters, March 23, 2022; Alex Mitchell, "Minimum Wage Would Be $61.75 if It Grew Like Wall Street Bonuses: Report," *New York Post,* March 24, 2022.

63 Jeanne Sahadi, "Wall Street Bonuses Hit Record High," CNN Business, March 23, 2022.

64 Christopher Flavelle, "U.S. to Pay Millions to Move Tribes Threatened by Climate Change," *New York Times,* November 30, 2022; Emma Newburger, "Biden Administration Grants $75 Million to Relocate Three Native Tribes Away from Rising Oceans," CNBC, November 30, 2022; Zack Budryk, "Biden Administration Paying $75 Million to Move Three Tribes Affected by Climate Change," The Hill, November 30, 2022.

65 Bella Kumar, "Accountable Allies: The Undue Influence of Fossil Fuel Money in Academia," Data for Progress, February 2023.

66 See, for example, Ilana Cohen and Michael E. Mann, "Climate Research Funded by Fossil Fuel Profits Discredits Universities and Hurts the Planet," *Los Angeles Times,* April 3, 2022; Hiroko Tabuchi, "Kicking Oil Companies Out of School," *New York Times,* August 16, 2022.

67 David Schechter, Chance Horner, and Aparna Zalani, "Is Your University Profiting From Climate Change?" CBS News, May 16, 2023.

68 See Zeinab Benchakroun and Susan Rahman, "Fossil Fuel Industry 'Colonizing' US Universities," story #21 from 2016-2017, accessible online in Project Censored's archive of its annual Top 25 story lists.

69 See, for example, "Infections Caught in Laboratories Are Surprisingly Common," *Economist,* April 24, 2021; Jon Gertner, "You Should Be Afraid of the Next 'Lab Leak'," *New York Times Magazine,* November 23, 2021; Tara Law, "Lab Leaks Are a Small But Real Risk in Ukraine. Russian Disinformation Is the True Threat," *Time,* March 29, 2022.

70 Joby Warrick and David Willman, "China's Struggles With Lab Safety Carry Danger of Another Pandemic," *Washington Post,* April 12, 2023.

71 Zeynep Tufekci, "The Pandemic Threat That Hasn't Gone Away," *New York Times,* May 12, 2023; Alison Young, "Dangerous Lab Leaks Happen Far More Often Than the Public Is Aware," *The Guardian,* May 30, 2023.

72 Emily L. Williams et al., "The American Electric Utility Industry's Role in Promoting Climate Denial, Doubt, and Delay," *Environmental Research Letters,* September 1, 2022.

73 See, for example, Geoffrey Supran and Naomi Oreskes, "What Exxon Mobil Didn't Say about Climate Change," *New York Times,* August 22, 2017; Michael Hiltzik, "A New Study Shows How Exxon Mobil Downplayed Climate Change When It Knew the Problem Was Real," *Los Angeles Times,* August 22, 2017.

74 Samuel R. Gross et al., "Race and Wrongful Convictions in the United States 2022," National Registry of Exonerations, September 2022.

75 Christina Swarns, "Op-Ed: Black People Are Wrongly Convicted More Than Any Other Group. We Can Prevent This," *Los Angeles Times*, October 7, 2022.

76 Kiara Alfonseca, "The Fight for Exoneration: Over 29,100 Years 'Lost' in Prison in Wrongful Convictions, Database Finds," ABC News, March 17, 2023.

77 Joseph Winters, "Puerto Rican Cities Sue Big Oil Over Climate Collusion," Grist, December 1, 2022; Nina Lakhani, "Big Oil Is Behind Conspiracy to Deceive Public, First Climate Racketeering Lawsuit Says," *The Guardian*, December 20, 2022; Ramenda Cyrus, "Puerto Rican Cities Sue Big Oil for Alleged Racketeering," *American Prospect*, January 25, 2023.

78 On DHS's Disinformation Governance Board, see also Andy Lee Roth and Mickey Huff, "Toward An American Ministry of Truth?" in *State of the Free Press 2023*, eds. Andy Lee Roth and Mickey Huff (Fair Oaks, CA and New York: Censored Press and Seven Stories Press, 2022), 11-14.

79 Tim Starks and Aaron Schaffer, "Look for Conservatives to Go After DHS Counter-Disinformation Work," *Washington Post*, November 3, 2022.

80 Kelly Laco, "Disinformation Push Shows DHS 'Politicizing' Itself, Say Top Homeland Security Republicans," Fox News, November 1, 2022; Adam Shaw, "Hawley Demands Answers on DHS 'Disinformation' Efforts, Accuses Mayorkas of Hiding Docs From Congress," Fox News, November 14, 2022.

81 Alec Schemmel, "Leaked Docs Show Facebook Made Portal for Feds to Report Misinfo, Report Says," ABC News (KRCR), October 31, 2022.

82 Ari Blaff, "Leaked Documents Reveal DHS Collaborated With Facebook to Target 'Disinformation'," *National Review*, October 31, 2022; John Hirschauer, "DHS's New Plan to Crack Down on 'Disinformation,'" *American Conservative*, November 1, 2022.

83 "Debt-Service Payments Put Biggest Squeeze on Poor Countries Since 2000," World Bank, December 6, 2022.

84 Carly Munnelly et al., "Fixing a Broken System: Transforming Global Education Financing," Save the Children, October 2022.

85 Gabriele Steinhauser and Alexander Saeedy, "Global Poor Lose Services as Developing Countries Face High Debt Payments," *Wall Street Journal*, November 29, 2022; Ana Monteiro, "Poorest Nations' Debt-Service Payments Surge 35% to $62 Billion," Bloomberg, December 6, 2022; Elliot Smith, "'We Should Be Worried': Finance Leaders Warn Rising Interest Rates Are Squeezing Low-Income Countries," CNBC, April 19, 2023; "Africa Faces A Mounting Debt Crisis," *Economist*, May 16, 2023.

86 Editorial Board, "Huge Debts to China Come Due. Will the World's Poorest Have to Pay?" *Washington Post*, February 22, 2023; Alan Rappeport, "Pressure Mounts on China to Offer Debt Relief to Poor Countries Facing Default," *New York Times*, April 14, 2023.

87 "The Economic Cost of Gun Violence," Everytown, July 19, 2022.

88 Zirui Song, José R. Zubizaretta, and Mia Giuriato, "Changes in Health Care Spending, Use, and Clinical Outcomes After Nonfatal Firearms Injuries Among Survivors and Family Members: A Cohort Study," *Annals of Internal Medicine* (June 2022).

89 "Gun Violence Archive 2023," Gun Violence Archive, May 31, 2023.
90 Everytown, "Economic Cost of Gun Violence."
91 Zirui Song, "The Business Case for Reducing Firearm Injuries," *Journal of the American Medical Association* 328, no. 12 (September 27, 2022): 1185-86. See also Phil B. Fontanarosa and Kirsten Bibbins-Domingo, "The Unrelenting Epidemic of Firearm Violence," *Journal of the American Medical Association* 328, no. 12 (September 27, 2022): 1201-3.
92 For instance, in May 2023, the *Los Angeles Times* ran a story about how fear of gun violence could put a damper on tourism revenues generated from the 2026 World Cup. See Kevin Baxter, "Mass Shootings and Gun Violence in U.S. Could Damage 2026 World Cup Bottom Line," *Los Angeles Times,* May 16, 2023.
93 "New Map Shows Toxic Chemical Releases, Fires and Explosions Occur Every Two Days on Average Across the U.S.," Coming Clean, February 25, 2023.
94 "Chemical Accident Prevention: EPA Should Ensure Regulated Facilities Consider Risks From Climate Change," United States Government Accountability Office, February 2022.
95 Max Graham, "A Spill Outside Philadelphia Adds to the Growing List of Chemical Accidents This Year," Grist, March 27, 2023.
96 Bruce D. Meyer et al., "Learning about Homelessness Using Linked Survey and Administrative Data," Becker Friedman Institute for Economics, Working Paper No. 2021-65, University of Chicago, June 3, 2021.
97 "Out of Reach 2022: The High Cost of Housing," National Low Income Housing Coalition, 2022.
98 Andrea Chang, "Low Wages, Short Hours Drive Many Fast-Food Workers Into Homelessness," *Los Angeles Times*, May 2, 2023; Elizabeth Napolitano, "Fast-Food Industry Drives Workers to Homelessness, Report Finds," CBS News, May 3, 2023.
99 Ruben Vives, "L.A. County Homeless Services Workers Can't Afford Housing Themselves, Study Finds," *Los Angeles Times*, May 15, 2023.
100 For Project Censored's previous coverage of this neglected news topic, see Yadira Martinez et al., "Antibiotic Resistant 'Superbugs' Threaten Health and Foundations of Modern Medicine," story #6 from 2016-2017; and Allison Rott and Steve Macek, "Antibiotic Abuse: Pharmaceutical Profiteering Accelerates Superbugs," story #19 from 2019-2020, both archived on the Project's website.
101 "Transcript: Ezra Klein Interviews Leah Garcés," *New York Times*, November 29, 2022.
102 Meaghan Cameron, "McDonald's and Taco Bell Still Use Beef That Is Putting Public Health at Risk, According to a New Investigation," EatThis, NotThat!, November 22, 2022; Margaret Darby, "McDonalds and Walmart Beef Suppliers Criticized for Antibiotic Overuse," *Deseret News*, November 23, 2022; "Reports Uncover 'Reckless' Antibiotic Use By McDonald's and Walmart Beef Suppliers," *Corporate Wellness Magazine*, December 8, 2022; The Editors, "To Fight Antimicrobial Resistance, Start With Farm Animals," *Scientific American*, March 1, 2023.
103 For example, WTOP News in Washington, DC, reported on suspensions of special education students in Fairfax County, Virginia: Scott Gelman,

"Fairfax Co. Special Education Students Disproportionately Suspended, Review Finds," WTOP News, October 3, 2022.

104   Erica L. Green, "How Educators Secretly Remove Students With Disabilities From School," *New York Times*, February 9, 2023.

105   Shannon Bond, "Elon Musk Is Using the Twitter Files to Discredit Foes and Push Conspiracy Theories," NPR, December 14, 2022; Charlie Warzel, "Elon Musk's Twitter Files Are Bait," *The Atlantic*, December 9, 2022; Aimee Picchi, "Twitter Files: What They Are and Why They Matter," CBS News, December 14, 2022.

106   "HIV Criminalization in the United States—Disproportional Impact," Williams Institute (UCLA School of Law), 2022.

107   Evelyn Mangold, "The Viral Injustice of HIV Criminalization," The Regulatory Review (University of Pennsylvania School of Law), February 24, 2022.

108   Jo Yurcaba, "Women Account for Two-Thirds of HIV-Related Arrests in Kentucky, Report Finds," NBC News, December 21, 2021.

109   "The Biden-Harris Administration Advances Equity and Opportunity for Black Americans and Communities Across the Country," The White House, press release, November 6, 2022.

CHAPTER 2

Déjà Vu News
What Happened to Previous *Censored* Stories

GRACE HARTY, KATHLEEN MINELLI,
NICOLE MENDEZ-VILLARRUBIA, and STEVE MACEK

Project Censored's central mission is to identify, investigate, and publicize consequential news stories reported on by the independent press that have been inadequately covered or ignored by corporate news media. Sometimes, the stories the Project spotlights receive belated coverage from major national commercial news outlets and eventually make their way into public discourse. In such instances, this is often because the conditions, facts, and larger issues highlighted by the original independent news coverage subsequently evolved in ways that rendered them impossible to ignore. However, even when the corporate media do begin giving these previously shunned stories some overdue coverage, all too often that coverage omits or downplays facts and perspectives that might prove embarrassing to the powers that be. More frequently, however, stories the Project has spotlighted never receive the wider media scrutiny they deserve. That is why this yearbook series includes this Déjà Vu News chapter, devoted to detailing the fates of stories from previous years' Top 25 lists.

This year's chapter updates important developments

and summarizes new independent and corporate media coverage for four past stories: From *Censored 2015*, we update story #22 about the corporate media's consistent minimization of rape and other forms of sexual abuse; from *Censored 2020*, we review story #8 on state "fetus protection" laws that criminalize miscarriage and stillbirth, a story that has taken on added significance in the wake of the Supreme Court's decision to overturn *Roe v. Wade*'s constitutional protections for abortion; we trace developments in the #1 story from *State of the Free Press 2021*, on murdered and missing Indigenous women and girls; and, lastly, we look back at story #6 from *State of the Free Press 2021*, about the growing network of conservative "pink slime" propaganda sites masquerading as local news outlets. As we show, the network of misleading websites analyzed in that story has only grown in size in the past three years.

Three of the four stories reviewed here concern women's rights and gendered violence. Each of the four demonstrates the power of independent media organizations such as *Ms. Magazine*, the Marshall Project, *Columbia Journalism Review*, and the UK's *Ceasefire Magazine* to raise awareness about injustice, spark broader discussion and protest, and sometimes even prompt urgently needed reforms.

Censored 2015 #22

Corporate News Understate Rape, Sexual Violence

Rania Khalek, "Calling Rape by Its Right Name," *Extra!* (Fairness and Accuracy in Reporting), February 1, 2014.

Wasi Daniju, "Dear Mainstream Media: I Believe the Word You're Looking For Is 'Rape,'" *Ceasefire Magazine*, November 10, 2013.

Eleanor J. Bader, "Stoking Fire: How News Outlets, Prosecutors Minimize Sexual Violence with Language," RH Reality Check, December 9, 2013.

Student Researchers: Cealia Brannan (Florida Atlantic University) and Laura A. Parada and Christina Sabia (Indian River State College)

Faculty Evaluators: James F. Tracy (Florida Atlantic University) and Elliot D. Cohen (Indian River State College)

In 2014, Project Censored identified the under- and misreporting of rape as one of the year's most significant but overlooked stories. Critics documented that corporate news media have tended to downplay rape and sexual violence in their reporting. Journalists use language such as "forced sex" and "inappropriate sexual activity" that detracts from the severity of the offenses they report.

Feminist advocacy group Legal Momentum, based in New York City, called this phenomenon "linguistic avoidance." Their August 2013 report, titled "Raped or 'Seduced'? How Language Helps Shape Our Response to Sexual Violence," explored how terms associated with consensual sex are used to describe assault. In such cases, the media misleads its audiences by portraying rape victims as willing participants.

A February 2014 article by Rania Khalek in *Extra!*, the magazine published by Fairness and Accuracy in Reporting (FAIR), cited an example from the *Los Angeles Times* in January 2013 as a case in point. Their story detailed how two Los Angeles police officers forced women they'd arrested to have sex with them under the threat of imprisonment. Legally, this is classified as rape, but the article did not use that word once. Instead, vague language diminished the horror of the crime.

Update

Since Project Censored first flagged this story in 2014, overall news coverage of sexual assault has risen in tandem with the prominence of the #MeToo movement. Nevertheless, a 2018 report by the Women's Media Center explained how the subject remains misrepresented and understated.[1] For example, reporters continued to use words such as "harassment" and "accuser" in their coverage of Harvey Weinstein even after the New York County District Attorney's Office officially charged him with rape and sexual assault. Instances like these reflect a larger culture of victim-blaming, according to an article by Women's eNews.[2] "Calling the alleged victims of sexual violence 'accusers' is an act of subtle but profound victim blaming that has the potential to silence future victims and set back the momentum of the growing anti-rape movement," Jackson Katz and Alison Bowen wrote. This language "reflects both pre-existing cultural biases about issues of male sexuality, sex and power, as well as deeply rooted misogyny and mistrust of women."

Publications including the *Columbia Journalism Review*, *Harvard Gazette*, and The Journalist's Resource covered a 2018 study examining the prevalence of rape culture in news media.[3] The authors of the study found that "where rape culture was more prevalent, there were more documented rape cases, but authorities were less vigilant in pursuing them."[4] The researchers also documented higher numbers of reported rapes in places where news coverage more frequently repeated elements of rape culture.

Statistics compiled by the Brennan Center for Justice highlight how many sexual assault survivors are hesitant to speak up. Only about 23 percent of survivors decide to file police reports.⁵ A culture of disbelief and victim-blaming keeps survivors, especially women, silent. The data also suggest fears of inaction by police and retaliation from society at large as contributing factors. According to the article's authors, "For all these reasons, unreported assaults are all too common. Far less common, however, are false accusations of sexual assault or rape, hovering between 2 and 10 percent in the United States . . . statistically speaking, it is far more common for a survivor of sexual assault to decline to report it than for someone to make false accusations of assault."

Additionally, news media frequently leave out sexual assault allegations and charges when reporting on prominent figures.⁶ Kobe Bryant, the basketball star who died in 2020, is a high-profile case in point. *The Washington Post* suspended a reporter who, a few hours after Bryant's death, tweeted a link to a Daily Beast article about the allegations against the former NBA all-star. Writer Felicia Sonmez gave no context in her original tweet, only elaborating after she received death threats that public figures should be remembered in their totality.⁷ Her follow-up tweet included a screenshot of the threatening and harassing messages sent to her via email. *The Washington Post* claimed Sonmez violated its social media policy and that her social media posts were undermining her colleagues' work. Sonmez explained that she posted the abusive email messages to show "the pressure people come under to stay silent in these cases."

When corporate media do address sexual assault allegations against celebrities, coverage is often disproportionate to the magnitude of the alleged crimes or the credibility of supporting evidence. In a June 2019 article for the *Columbia Journalism Review*, Jon Allsop argued that *Elle* magazine columnist E. Jean Carroll's allegation that Donald Trump raped her in a Bergdorf Goodman dressing room in 1995 or 1996 had not received nearly the attention it deserved.[8] As Allsop pointed out, Carroll's description of the incident was "graphic and detailed" and "corroborated by two friends who recall Carroll telling them about it at the time," earning front-page coverage in *New York Magazine* but remarkably little coverage by other national news outlets. The story failed to make the front pages of the *New York Times, Wall Street Journal, Los Angeles Times*, and *Chicago Tribune*. Although the story appeared on the front page of the *Washington Post*, it wasn't the newspaper's lead story. Furthermore, the *New York Post* took down an article detailing the charges hours after it had been posted. Carroll's account of Trump's actions only made headlines after May 9, 2023, when a jury found him liable for battery, sexual abuse, and defamation and awarded Carroll damages of $5 million.[9]

Gaps in reporting on sexual assault are not surprising when news corporations themselves fail to create safe, equitable work environments for women. According to the 2018 Women's Media Center report, nearly two-thirds of female journalists experience sexual harassment or violence at work. The Center's report on #MeToo and the media described "an outpouring of accusations against men at every level, including the very top of media organizations. The number of powerful men dethroned ... publicly betrays a previously silent, pervasive climate of sexual intimidation and assault within the press."[10] Rather than scrutinize itself, the corporate media's coverage of sexual assault often focuses on other industries.

Banishing rape culture from the corporate media is easier said than done. To begin, reporters and readers alike must call it out by name and create an environment where survivors are supported. Women must also have a fair share of power in the industry. The leadership of most media organizations, especially at the top, skews heavily in favor of White men.[11] The pattern affects rank-and-file media workers as well, with White women holding only 33 percent of entry-level positions and women of color holding a mere 17 percent of them. As Project Censored's Shealeigh Voitl and Steve Macek argued in an April 2022 article for *Ms. Magazine*, "There simply cannot be inclusive coverage without an inclusive staff. Hiring women and journalists of color allows news organizations to report stories that better address the needs and interests of the communities they serve."

Censored 2020 #8

US Women Face Prison Sentences for Miscarriages

Naomi Randolph, "What Losing Roe Would Mean for Women of Color," *Ms. Magazine*, January 22, 2019.

Student Researcher: Abby Ehrler (North Central College)

Faculty Evaluator: Steve Macek (North Central College)

In 2019, many observers feared that the new conservative Supreme Court majority would overturn *Roe v. Wade*, stripping women of the right to control their reproductive health. If this happened, Naomi Randolph argued in a 2019 *Ms. Magazine* article, pregnant women could potentially face a higher risk of criminal charges for miscarriages or stillbirths, due to laws in numerous states that recognize fetuses as people, separate from the women carrying them.

As an example of the dangers women would face in a post-Roe United States, Randolph pointed to Alabama, where voters had passed a measure that endowed the fetus "with 'personhood' rights for the first time, potentially making any action that impacts a fetus a criminal behavior with potential for prosecution." In Arkansas, Anne Bynum was convicted of "concealing a birth" when she delivered a stillborn child at her home in 2015, per an Arkansas statute that left women vulnerable to conviction if they waited even a minute before contacting authorities.

The commonality in each of these cases is that women lost their rights because they were endangering a fetus. Randolph detailed that this especially hurts women of color and low-income women, due to "limited access to contraception and affordable health care."

Without constitutional protection for the right to an abortion, Randolph argued, the criminalization of miscarriages could become an even bigger problem. As she explained, proposed changes to the Affordable Care Act would "allow employers to deny women no-cost birth control based on [employers'] religious and 'moral' beliefs." This followed proposals to limit funding to Planned Parenthood. Randolph cautioned that Trump's 2018 Supreme Court Justice appointee, Brett Kavanaugh, "would be the fifth vote necessary to overturn *Roe v. Wade,* opening the door to criminalizing women for the reproductive decisions they make."

The New York Times was the only corporate source that discussed the possibility of women being prosecuted for pregnancy loss. However, the *Times* only touched on it in opinion pieces—including, notably, a December 2018 editorial titled "A Woman's Rights"—rather than as a topic featured in headlines and news stories.[12] This issue has mainly been covered by independent news sources such as *Ms. Magazine* and Rewire News Group.

Update

In June 2022, the US Supreme Court's controversial ruling in *Dobbs v. Jackson Women's Health Organization* overturned *Roe v. Wade*, taking away women's constitutional right to abortion. Since this judicial setback for a woman's bodily autonomy and freedom of choice, many of the fears about the criminalization of miscarriages articulated in Randolph's 2019 *Ms. Magazine* article have been realized.

In the past four years, more and more women have faced criminal prosecution following a pregnancy loss, especially in states with fetal-protection laws, such as Alabama, Oklahoma, and South Carolina. Many of these prosecutions blame women's drug use as the cause of their fetuses' deaths, despite the complexity involved in determining the causes of miscarriages and stillbirths.

Even before the *Dobbs* ruling, in November 2021, BBC News ran a story about Brittney Poolaw, a 21-year-old Oklahoma woman convicted of manslaughter after having a miscarriage in 2020.[13] The BBC reported that Poolaw, who miscarried only sixteen to seventeen weeks into her term, was the earliest-term pregnant woman to ever be charged for having a miscarriage. According to a medical examiner, her unborn son had traces of methamphetamine in his liver and brain, although the cause of his death was officially undetermined. Poolaw was sentenced to four years in prison. As the BBC reported, the National Advocates of Pregnant Women, now known as Pregnancy Justice, documented more than 1,600 arrests and cases of "forcible intervention" against pregnant women in the United States between 1973 to 2020. The BBC's report emphasized how many of these cases involved women who miscarried due to events such as giving birth at home or even falling.

Cases like Poolaw's have become even more common since *Dobbs*. In a September 2022 article posted by the Marshall Project, Amy Yurkanin covered the story of Brooke Shoemaker, a mother of four sentenced to prison for drug use that allegedly harmed her fetus.[14] Shoemaker was arrested two months after delivering a stillborn baby and charged with chemical endangerment causing death, a law only enforced in Alabama. While in the hospital following her miscarriage, she admitted to a doctor that she had used methamphetamine and spoke with a detective. Though a pathologist concluded that the cause of death of the fetus was "undetermined," the coroner—an elected official with no medical training—put "chemical endangerment" as the cause of death on the death certificate. A jury ultimately found Shoemaker guilty and she was sentenced to eighteen years in prison. According to Yurkanin, "Shoemaker is among at least 20 women in Alabama since 2006 who suffered miscarriage or stillbirth—then had to face the harshest possible criminal charges, with consequences as severe as those for murder, rape or kidnapping."

According to an article by Cary Aspinwall, Brianna Bailey, and Amy Yurkanin, also published by the Marshall

Project in September 2022, since 1999, more than fifty women have been prosecuted for child neglect or more serious crimes after testing positive for drugs following a miscarriage.[15] Yet, as they wrote, "There isn't scientific proof that using methamphetamine or other drugs causes pregnancy loss." As they explained, women who have used drugs deliver healthy babies every day.

Perhaps the most outrageous case involved a woman who was not even pregnant. As Shira Li Bartov reported in a November 2022 article for *Newsweek,* Stacey Freeman, a resident of Gallant, Alabama, was being investigated by the Etowah County Department of Human Resources in January 2022 for possible drug use when one of her daughters told an investigator that Freeman was pregnant.[16] Though Freeman insisted she wasn't pregnant and was menstruating at the time, she was arrested for "chemical endangerment of a child" and held in jail for thirty-six hours. She eventually underwent a pregnancy test—which came back negative—and was allowed to leave, but only after a sheriff's investigator "threatened, warned, and admonished Freeman" that she would be charged if it was discovered that she was pregnant any time in the next several months.

In their Marshall Project article, Aspinwall, Bailey, and Yurkanin pointed out that many of the women convicted of crimes involving stillbirths or miscarriages are poor and struggling with substance abuse problems. They wrote that these women's prosecutions result in "lengthy prison sentences and life-altering consequences." Moreover, they noted, "Women sent to prison after pregnancy loss are among the few Americans serving time for drug consumption; most laws criminalize drug possession and sales, not use."[17]

In the wake of the *Dobbs* decision, the corporate media have provided some coverage of women being imprisoned for miscarriages or for using drugs while pregnant, including, in the past year, reports from NPR, ABC, the *Washington Post,* and *Marie Claire.*[18] Yet these prosecutions are so outrageous that they arguably deserve far more attention than received to date.

State of the Free Press 2021 #1

Missing and Murdered Indigenous Women and Girls

Danielle McLean, "Missing and Murdered Women Is a Grim, Unsolved Problem. Native Communities Are Demanding Action," ThinkProgress, August 24, 2019.

Abaki Beck, "Why Aren't Fossil Fuel Companies Held Accountable for Missing and Murdered Indigenous Women?" *YES! Magazine*, October 5, 2019.

Hallie Golden, "'Sister, Where Did You Go?': The Native American Women Disappearing from US Cities," *The Guardian*, May 1, 2019.

Carrie N. Baker, "Making Missing and Murdered Indigenous Women and Girls Visible," *Ms. Magazine*, December 2, 2019. Originally published as "Speaking Out Carrie Baker: Invisible No More: Native American Women and Girls on Thanksgiving," *Daily Hampshire Gazette*, November 27, 2019.

Student Researchers: Jeramy Dominguez (Sonoma State University), Katrina Tend (Diablo Valley College), and James Byers (Frostburg State University)

Faculty Evaluators: Ashley Hall (Sonoma State University), Mickey Huff (Diablo Valley College), and Andy Duncan (Frostburg State University)

Indigenous women and girls face physical violence—including murder, kidnapping, sexual trafficking, and rape—with a "shocking regularity" that amounts to an "epidemic" of violence, according to an August 2019 report from ThinkProgress. (Here and following, our use of the terms "women and girls" includes those who identify as Two-Spirit, lesbian, gay, bisexual, transgender, queer, questioning, intersex, or asexual.) The scope of the problem is "almost impossible to put into context," the *Guardian* reported in May 2019, because no single federal government database consistently tracks how many Native women and girls go missing each year. Due to negligence, incapacity, and the complexity of criminal jurisdiction on tribal lands, law enforcement seldom identifies the perpetrators of these crimes, much less charge or convict them.

As ThinkProgress reported, the Urban Indian Health Institute found 5,712 reports of murdered or missing Native women and girls throughout the United States in 2016—but only 116 of these were logged in the Department of Justice's database. According to Federal Bureau of Investigation data, Native Americans disappear at twice the per capita rate of White Americans, while research funded by the Department of Justice found that on some tribal lands, Indigenous women were murdered at more than ten times the national average, the *Guardian* reported. A 2016 Department of Justice report, based on 2010 data, found that "more than 4 in 5 American Indian and Alaska Native women (84.3 percent) have experienced violence in their lifetime," and more than one in three (34.1 percent) have experienced rape.

"I wouldn't say we're more vulnerable," Annita Lucchesi, executive director of the Sovereign Bodies Institute, told the *Guardian*, "I'd say we're targeted."

Activist groups, including the Sovereign Bodies Institute, the Brave Heart Society, and the Urban Indian Health Institute, identified aspects of systemic racism as deep-rooted sources of the crisis.

Update

More than two years since the original articles were published, establishment news outlets are finally covering the crisis of murdered and missing Indigenous women (MMIW) in the United States. Articles published in widely-circulated newspapers such as *USA Today* now highlight the previous lack of attention to the crisis.[19] Multiple major news sources, including the *New York Times* and the *Los Angeles Times*, have published articles addressing the lack of attention to and support for Indigenous women and girls and their families.[20]

Various factors have contributed to this shift in news coverage, including, as Minnesota Lt. Gov. Peggy Flanagan told *U.S. News & World Report*, the "historic number of native women across the country running for office and serving in positions" in 2020.[21] President Biden's appointment of the first Native American Secretary of the Interior, Deb Haaland, has also had an impact; in April 2021, Haaland created a new unit within the Bureau of Indian Affairs dedicated to investigating missing and murdered Native Americans.[22] At the grassroots level, Native Americans, particularly Native women, have also been creating and leading gatherings and marches to bring attention to the silence surrounding the disappearance and murder of Native women. For example, as the *Christian Science Monitor* reported, Meskee Yatsayte hosts Navajo Nation Missing Persons Updates, a Facebook page that posts flyers of women and girls who have disappeared and provides updates on previously posted cases.[23]

State governments are beginning to develop programs to address the MMIW crisis. In 2020, for example, Wisconsin and Utah established task forces charged with fighting violence against and abduction of Indigenous women; in 2021, South Dakota and Oklahoma created entire offices to address missing Indigenous people. Also in 2021, Kansas enacted a law that would pave the way for relevant police training to help with the crisis, and the Washington state attorney general announced that he would be leading a task force as well. "Lawmakers and attorneys general have played key roles in creation of the task forces. Most have two goals: to address the scope of the problem and make recommendations for how to remedy it. They tend to consist primarily of lawmakers, tribal representatives, law enforcement officials, and advocates and service providers for Indigenous women and girls," *U.S. News & World Report* explained in a November 2021 article.[24]

Perhaps more importantly, in 2021 and 2022, the Biden White House declared May 5 Missing or Murdered Indigenous Persons Awareness Day.[25] In his 2022 proclamation, President Biden announced that the Department of Justice had started working closely with Tribal Nations to develop "regionally appropriate guidelines" for resolving investigations of missing or murdered Indigenous people. Biden also touted the enactment of the Violence Against Women Act Reauthorization Act of 2022, which extended the special criminal jurisdiction of Tribal courts to hold non-Native perpetrators accountable for sexual assault, child abuse, stalking, sex trafficking, and assaults on Tribal law enforcement officers that take place on Tribal lands. "My Administration understands that Native people, particularly survivors of violence, know best what their communities need to feel safe. That is why we must work hand in hand with Tribal partners through each phase of the justice system to create solutions that are victim-centered, trauma-informed, and culturally appropriate," President Biden asserted.[26]

Corporate news media and the political establishment have finally begun to pay attention to the national crisis of murdered and missing Indigenous women and girls.[27] However, it should be noted that this shift in coverage happened two to three years after independent news coverage in outlets such as the *Guardian, YES! Magazine*, and *Ms. Magazine*. If major establishment news outlets had reported on the MMIW crisis earlier, perhaps this progress could have occurred sooner and fewer people would have suffered.

State of the Free Press 2021 #6

Shadow Network of Conservative Outlets Emerges to Exploit Faith in Local News

Priyanjana Bengani, "Hundreds of 'Pink Slime' Local News Outlets are Distributing Algorithmic Stories and Conservative Talking Points," *Columbia Journalism Review*, December 18, 2019.

Carol Thompson, "Dozens of New Websites Appear to Be Michigan Local News Outlets, but with Political Bent," *Lansing State Journal*, October 20, 2019, updated October 22, 2019.

Student Researcher: Troy Patton (Diablo Valley College)

Faculty Evaluator: Mickey Huff (Diablo Valley College)

A December 2019 report by the *Columbia Journalism Review* highlighted how a network of 450 websites operated by five companies in twelve states "mimic the appearance and output of traditional news organizations" in order to "manipulate public opinion by exploiting faith in local media." These sites "co-opt the language, design and structure of news organizations," Priyanjana Bengani reported, to "cover certain candidates and topics, including limited government, tort reform, and labor unions, with a conservative bias."

The story of "[d]ozens of websites branded as local news outlets" in Michigan, a crucial swing state in the 2016 election, was originally reported by Carol Thompson for the *Lansing State Journal* in October 2019. The *CJR* report expanded on previous investigations conducted by Thompson and others, which had identified around two hundred sites in several states posing as local news outlets while publishing politically biased content.

Thompson's original report for the *Lansing State Journal* noted that the network of websites in Michigan shared a common "About Us" section, identifying Metric Media as the publisher and describing its plans to launch thousands of such sites nationwide. The sites' privacy policy pages indicated that they were all operated by Locality Labs, which operates similar networks of sites in Illinois and Maryland and identified Brian Timpone as Locality Labs's CEO.

Although the web of interconnected sites is difficult to follow, the *CJR* highlighted five corporate bodies with twenty-one news networks that were connected through a complex web of shared IP addresses, backend web IDs, and the involvement of Timpone. As *CJR* reported, "In 2012, Timpone's company Journatic, an outlet known for its low-cost automated story generation (which became known as "pink slime journalism"), attracted national attention and outrage for faking bylines and quotes, and for plagiarism."[28] In 2013, Journatic rebranded as Locality Labs.

Brian Timpone is also the co-founder of Local Government Information Services (LGIS), a network of more than thirty print and web publications in Illinois that feature conservative news and share the same layout as Metric Media's websites. And, as *CJR* reported, in 2015, Timpone incorporated Newsinator, a firm that the *Chicago Tribune* described as having a history of "doing paid political work and offer[ing] marketing services to companies under the name Interactive Content Services."[29] The CEO of Franklin Archer, which operates the single largest network of these faux-local publications, is Michael Timpone, Brian's brother.

At the time Project Censored reported this story, several scholarly books on growing control over local media outlets by conservative owners with ties to rightwing organizations had been published.[30] Yet major corporate news outlets provided only minimal coverage of this topic. In October 2019, the *New York Times* published a piece that credited the *Lansing State Journal* with breaking the story on pseudo-local news organizations in Michigan and drew significantly from Carol Thompson's original report. *The Columbia Journalism Review*'s piece expanded on the breadth and scope of previous coverage, but at the time Project Censored's *State of the Free Press 2021* went to press, the *CJR*'s findings had not been reported by any of the big establishment news outlets.

Update

Since *CJR*'s initial investigation of pink slime sites in December 2019, hyper-partisan websites and print publications masquerading as local news outlets have continued to proliferate.

A follow-up investigation by *CJR* found that by August 2020, the conservative pink slime network had tripled in size to encompass more than 1,200 websites.[31] Further research published by *CJR* in October 2021 documented that a majority of these sites received the bulk of their funding from rightwing dark money organizations such as Donors Trust, CatholicVote.org, and the National Christian Charitable Foundation.[32]

As the sprawling network of dubious rightwing "local news" websites has expanded, corporate media have begun to pay attention.

In a December 2022 *Chicago Tribune* op-ed, News-Guard executive director Jim Warren claimed that his organization had "identified 1,202 of these so-called 'pink slime' outlets across the country, slightly less than the 1,230 daily newspapers left operating in the U.S. The right- and left-leaning sites blossom as traditional newspapers disappear at a rate of two per week."[33]

As the *Washington Post* noted in an October 2022 editorial, many of the newly created conservative websites were launched immediately "before the 2020 elections to bolster Republican campaigns."[34] *The Post* editorial pointed out that in the lead-up to the 2021 Virginia gubernatorial election, the Popular Information Substack counted 4,657 articles published by these sites on the dangers of critical race theory—a key theme of Republican gubernatorial candidate Glenn Youngkin.

Illinois saw an explosion of rightwing "pink slime" sites and printed propaganda sheets made to look like newspapers during the state's 2022 gubernatorial election. In June 2022, the *Washington Post* and *Chicago Tribune* each spotlighted how a completely fabricated story, about school officials in Oak Park, Illinois, supposedly adopting race-based grading, went viral.[35] The false story was initially "reported" by a bogus conservative news site based in Chicago and later circulated far more widely by national conservative media such as Newsmax. Shortly before election day, NPR ran an exposé by media reporter David Folkenflik about how Dan Proft, a conservative talk show host and former fellow at the far-right Illinois Policy Institute, had created a network of "pink slime" publications and websites across the state with $40 million in backing from Republican businessman Dick Uihlein. As Folkenflik observed, the fake newspapers published by Profit's outlets, which flooded Illinois voters' mailboxes during the recent election, made no disclosures about their agenda or partisan connections, making them clear examples of dishonest "advocacy laundering."[36]

To be fair, the tactic of using faux news sites to promote partisan propaganda is not exclusive to conservatives. "Democrats are starting to play the pink slime game as well," Ryan Zickgraf pointed out in an October 2022 essay for *Jacobin*.[37] Although not nearly as well-funded or all-pervasive as their rightwing counterparts, Democratic-leaning sites masquerading as authentic local news sources are now operating in Michigan and Arizona.

Interestingly, recent research indicates that the millions of dark money dollars being poured into pink slime websites across the political spectrum may all be for naught. A 2023 Stanford University study of Americans' web browsing activities in the months leading up to the 2020 elections found a "mismatch between production and consumption" of partisan pink slime reporting. Only 3.7 percent of Americans were exposed to pink slime, the study found, and few actually paid attention to the most heavily promoted topics.[38]

GRACE HARTY is a senior majoring in Communication Studies and minoring in Writing at North Central College in Naperville, IL. She plans on following her dreams as a writer after she graduates.

KATHLEEN MINELLI graduated with a degree in English Writing from North Central College in May 2023 and will be attending graduate school in the fall.

NICOLE MENDEZ-VILLARRUBIA is a senior majoring in Journalism and Media Communication, with minors in Gender and Sexuality Studies and Sociology, at North Central College. Her writing can be found in the *Chronicle*, NCC's award-winning student news publication. She believes the media can be a powerful tool for elevating diverse voices and social causes.

STEVE MACEK is a Professor of Communication and Media studies at North Central College and serves as co-coordinator of Project Censored's Campus Affiliates Program. He writes frequently about censorship and First Amendment issues for Truthout, Common Dreams, and other independent media outlets.

Notes

1   Eliza Ennis and Lauren Wolfe, "Media and #MeToo: The Women's Media Center Report," Women's Media Center, October 5, 2018.
2   Jackson Katz and Alison Bowen, "Let's Stop Calling Bill Cosby's Victims 'Accusers'," Women's eNews, January 21, 2015.
3   Meg Dalton, "Is the News Media Complicit in Spreading Rape Culture?" *Columbia Journalism Review*, October 26, 2018; Christina Pazzanese, "How Rape Culture Shapes Whether a Survivor Is Believed," *Harvard Gazette*, August 25, 2020; Denise-Marie Ordway, "'Where There Is

More Rape Culture in the Press, There Is More Rape'," The Journalist's Resource, September 7, 2018.

4 Matthew A. Baum, Dara Kay Cohen, and Yuri M. Zhukov, "Does Rape Culture Predict Rape? Evidence from U.S. Newspapers, 2000–2013," *Quarterly Journal of Political Science* 13, no. 3 (August 30, 2018): 263-89.

5 Cameron Kimble and Inimai M. Chettiar, "Sexual Assault Remains Dramatically Underreported," Brennan Center for Justice, October 4, 2018.

6 Christina Cauterucci, "How Media Outlets Are Acknowledging (And Not Acknowledging) Kobe Bryant's Rape Case," Slate, January 27, 2020.

7 EJ Dickson, "Why Did the Washington Post Suspend a Reporter After She Tweeted About Kobe Bryant's Rape Allegation?" *Rolling Stone*, January 27, 2020.

8 Jon Allsop, "E. Jean Carroll's Trump Rape Claim Did Not Get Enough Coverage," *Columbia Journalism Review*, June 24, 2019.

9 Lauren Del Valle, "Jury Finds Trump Sexually Abused E. Jean Carroll in Civil Case, Awards Her $5 Million," CNN, May 10, 2023; Maggie Haberman and Jonathan Swan, "For Trump, a Verdict That's Harder to Spin," *New York Times,* May 10, 2023.

10 Ennis and Wolfe, "Media and #MeToo."

11 Steve Macek and Shealeigh Voitl, "'The News That Didn't Make the News': How the Media Ignores Important Stories About Gender Violence and Inequity," *Ms. Magazine*, April 4, 2022.

12 Editorial Board, "A Woman's Rights," *New York Times*, December 28, 2018.

13 Robin Levinson-King, "US Women Are Being Jailed for Having Miscarriages," BBC, November 12, 2021.

14 Amy Yurkanin, "She Lost Her Baby, Then Her Freedom," Marshall Project, September 1, 2022.

15 Cary Aspinwall, Brianna Bailey, and Amy Yurkanin, "They Lost Their Pregnancies. Then Prosecutors Sent Them To Prison," Marshall Project, September 1, 2022.

16 Shira Li Bartov, "A Woman Was Jailed for 'Endangering' Her Fetus— She Wasn't Even Pregnant," *Newsweek,* November 22, 2022.

17 Aspinwall, Bailey, and Yurkanin, "They Lost Their Pregnancies."

18 Robert Baldwin III, "Losing a Pregnancy Could Land You in Jail in Post-Roe America," *All Things Considered* (NPR), July 3, 2022; Devin Dwyer and Patty See, "Prosecuting Pregnancy Loss: Why Advocates Fear a Post-Roe Surge of Charges," ABC News, September 28, 2022; Marisa Iati, "Pregnant Women Were Jailed Over Drug Use to Protect Fetuses, County Says," *Washington Post*, September 8, 2022.

19 Nora Mabie, "A Crisis Ignored: Why Are People Turning a Blind Eye to Missing Indigenous Women?" interview by James Brown, *USA Today*, May 22, 2022.

20 Jack Healy, "Rural Montana Had Already Lost Too Many Native Women. Then Selena Disappeared," *New York Times*, January 20, 2020, updated January 22, 2020; Hannah Wiley, "Trying to Break the Chain of Missing Indigenous Women," *Los Angeles Times*, March 20, 2023.

21 Devon Haynie, "How States Are Addressing Violence Against Indigenous Women," *U.S. News & World Report,* November 1, 2021.

22 Ryan Grenoble, "The Interior Department Is Finally Getting Serious About Missing, Murdered Native Americans," HuffPost, April 2, 2021.

23 Henry Gass, "Missing Indigenous Women: Activists Spur a Reckoning," *Christian Science Monitor*, June 6, 2022.

24 Haynie, "How States Are Addressing Violence Against Indigenous Women."

25 Joseph R. Biden, Jr., "A Proclamation on Missing and Murdered Indigenous Persons Awareness Day, 2021," The White House, May 4, 2021; and Joseph R. Biden, Jr., "A Proclamation on Missing or Murdered Indigenous Persons Awareness Day, 2022," The White House, May 4, 2022.

26 Biden, Jr., "A Proclamation on Missing or Murdered Indigenous Persons Awareness Day, 2022."

27 Some notable examples of recent corporate media coverage include Tenzin Shakya, "Searching for Missing Indigenous Women, Tribes and Lawmakers Seek to Raise Awareness," ABC News, May 8, 2023; and Cheyanne M. Daniels, "Day of Awareness Puts Focus On Missing and Murdered Indigenous Women," The Hill, May 5, 2023.

28 Ryan Smith, a freelance reporter who worked for Journatic, coined the term "pink slime journalism." See Anna Tarkov, "Journatic Worker Takes 'This American Life' Inside Outsourced Journalism," Poynter, June 30, 2012.

29 Joe Mahr, "Conservative Illinois Publications Blur Lines Between Journalism, Politics," *Chicago Tribune*, April 6, 2018.

30 See Anne Nelson, *Shadow Network: Media, Money, and the Secret Hub of the Radical Right* (New York: Bloomsbury Publishing, 2019); Katherine Stewart, *The Power Worshippers: Inside the Dangerous Rise of Religious Nationalism* (New York: Bloomsbury Publishing, 2020); and Andrew L. Whitehead and Samuel L. Perry, *Taking America Back for God: Christian Nationalism in the United States* (New York: Oxford University Press, 2020).

31 Priyanjana Bengani, "As Election Looms, a Network of Mysterious 'Pink Slime' Local News Sites Nearly Triples in Size," *Columbia Journalism Review*, August 4, 2020.

32 Priyanjana Bengani, "The Metric Media Network Runs More Than 1,200 Local News Sites. Here Are Some of the Non-profits Funding Them," *Columbia Journalism Review*, October 14, 2021.

33 Jim Warren, "Fake Newspapers Are Everywhere and on Both Sides of the Political Divide," *Chicago Tribune*, December 10, 2022.

34 Editorial Board, "Hyperpartisan 'Local News' Sites Are Dangerous to Democracy," *Washington Post*, October 23, 2022.

35 Margret Sullivan, "Beware Partisan 'Pink Slime' Sites That Pose as Local News," *Washington Post*, June, 5, 2022; John Keilman, "Race, Politics and Misinformation Combine as False Story About Oak Park and River Forest High School Grading Goes Viral," *Chicago Tribune*, June 2, 2022.

36 David Folkenflik, "Right-wing 'Zombie' Papers Attack Illinois Democrats Ahead of Elections," *Morning Edition* (NPR), October 31, 2022.

37 Ryan Zickgraf, "As Serious Local Journalism Declines, Empty Partisan Hackery Is Taking Its Place," *Jacobin*, October 19, 2022.

38 See the preprint of the Stanford study here: Ryan Christopher Moore et al., "The Consumption of Pink Slime Journalism: Who, What, When,

Where, and Why?" ResearchGate, February 2023; as reported by Mark Caro, "As 'Pink Slime' Aims to Fill Local News Vacuum, Is Anyone Reading?" Local News Initiative (Northwestern University), March 28, 2023.

CHAPTER 3

Repurpose, Recycle, Reuse

**All the Junk Food News We Couldn't Refuse . . .
So Here's a Buffet!**

JEN LYONS, SIERRA KAUL, REAGAN HAYNIE, MARCELLE
LEVINE SWINBURNE, GAVIN KELLEY, and MICKEY HUFF

Over the years, Americans have proven to prefer "Junk Food" clickbait headlines over news stories with actual intellectual, nutritional value. Lucky for them, this year's Junk Food News spread leaves no crumbs behind. "Junk Food News," a term originally coined by Project Censored founder Carl Jensen in 1983, is an umbrella expression used to describe a category of frivolous or inconsequential news stories that receive substantial coverage by corporate news outlets, thus distracting audiences from other, more significant stories.[1] Instead of serving up nutritionally dense narratives—news you can use, like the stories in Chapter 1 of this book—corporate outlets prefer to dumpster dive for Twinkie equivalent soundbites, creating a never-ending buffet of celebrity gossip, vapid commentary, and other diversions from reality. These stories are so lackluster and nutrient deficient that they'll surely leave you hungry for more.

This year, we're kicking off the chapter by going green. The Project Censored team is embarking on a mission to repurpose, recycle, and reuse some of the Junk Food News menu items from the past. If the corporate media can do it, why can't we? While these leftovers may seem stale, they're still among millions of Americans' favorite guilty junk news snacks. All our favorites are back, including Keeping Up with Ye and the Kardashians' junk, junkyard professional sports drama, and space junk billionaire Elon Musk. Even Pamela Anderson found her way back into headlines regarding the illegal distribution of her 1990s sex tape with Mötley Crüe rocker Tommy Lee—can't get more recycled than that. In fact, there were so many Junk-related news stories that this year we had to serve up a buffet of endless options just waiting to fill your plate.

Need a glimpse at the menu before you decide? We've got you covered! This year's grazing experience includes a delicious three-course meal even before the buffet is set! Got a hankering for YouTuber-driven healthcare initiatives? What about foreign spy operations and UFO conspiracies? If that doesn't satisfy your tastebuds, the latest NBA scandal will surely leave you coming back for more. Also, don't worry about overeating—we've got the perfect solution. *Cue the Ozempic® ad!* We hope you came hungry, ready to binge and purge on some piping hot Junk Food News.

FAUX-LANTHROPY: MRBEAST AND THE BEASTLY REALITY OF AMERICAN HEALTHCARE

Online "influencers" continue to gain notoriety as more and more individuals make names for themselves on platforms like Instagram, TikTok, and YouTube. Given that millions of people vie for online attention doing whatever their schtick may be or sharing whatever hot take they want to share, some are trying to do good in the world, or so they claim. Take Jimmy Donaldson, more widely known as YouTube celebrity "MrBeast," the most subscribed person on YouTube. On January 28, 2023, he released a video wherein he paid for the procedure to cure blindness in a thousand people, donated money for more people to be cured, and even gave away a Tesla to one of the cured participants.[2] Immediately, the internet was abuzz about MrBeast's generosity. Most of his other videos are based on insane challenges. For example, "$456,000 Squid Game in Real Life" and "Last to Leave Circle Wins $500,000" are his most-watched releases with 364 and 261 million views respectively.[3] In comparison, the aforementioned video, in which MrBeast helps cure blindness in a thousand people, currently sits at a meager 145 million views, as opposed to dozens of his more popular videos. Apparently, people would rather watch others sit in a stationary circle to win money than watch vision-impaired people see for the first time. Eyes on the prize, if you will?

That said, MrBeast received almost immediate backlash for publishing this particular video. As much as the internet was in awe of the content creator and his charitable actions, there were a great many who were equally angry at his advertisement-riddled YouTube video, from which he would inherently profit. It is estimated that MrBeast makes between $500,000 to $1 million from ad revenue alone per video he releases. Additionally, if the video itself is sponsored by some company hawking a product, he can make even more. Recent estimates put his net worth at $54 million in 2021.[4] As the updated saying goes, an eye for an eye makes the whole world blind, but paying seven grand for eye surgery can make you millions on YouTube. When faced with this backlash, MrBeast responded on Twitter, saying he did not even understand why blindness "was a thing" if, as the doctor in his video said, it could be cured in about 50 percent of the people it affects.[5] Oh, MrBeast, how do you not know that health-care is not designed for our health? Turns out one doesn't need to understand America's general for-profit disease management system (cough . . . healthcare) to become a YouTube sensation.

This "healthcare system" in the United States rakes in trillions of dollars a year, both from insurance companies and non-insured people. Individual hospitals can set their prices for services and supplies and keep these prices in what is known as a "chargemaster." Typically, these med-ical prices are kept a secret, but California requires that hospitals in the state record their prices with the depart-ment and have them published. To illustrate this, a bag of IV fluid used to go for $137 in-house, when it costs less than a dollar to manufacture. Now, however, it can cost up to $500. Additionally, the average 200 milligrams (mg) aspirin tablet would cost fifteen cents when bought from the local pharmacy. It can range from $11 to $19 per tablet at various hospitals.[6] But like an opposite-day Porky Pig, *that's not all folks*! A vial of anesthetic can go for almost $80, while it can be bought online for a measly five bucks. And while some hospitals in California have cheaper prices, it can be difficult to shop for a discounted medical experience when one needs immediate care.[7] MrBeast's next challenge video should be him trying to influence the chargemasters to lower their prices.

The most perplexing issue regarding MrBeast's com-ment about curable blindness still being a "thing" is how he said he did not understand why the government would not step in to help. Well, some governments *have* helped with surgeries to correct curable blindness—just not the United States government. The Venezuelan and Cuban governments created Operación Milagro (Miracle Mission) in 2004 in hopes of helping with curable blindness internationally. They have provided millions of procedures free of charge in Latin America since their inception (side-eye to MrBeast). In fact, they had already completed at least two million correction surgeries within their first seven years of operation in thirty countries worldwide.[8] Notably, the United States is not a part of the outreach for Operación Milagro, especially given how the US government has ignored Cuban welfare before. Fun fact: Cuba attempted to send aid to Hurricane Katrina victims in the US before FEMA even began to act but was rebuffed by the George W. Bush administration.[9]

It's not that the United States doesn't have the resources to help with curable blindness in its citizens. It's that it is not profitable to give away medical care for free. Why give something away when someone could buy it? Oh, a cure is unaffordable? Perhaps you should have thought before suffering an injury or illness that cannot be remedied with a band-aid or a cough drop. In the US, the healthcare system is no charitable enterprise. It's a booming business where profits matter more than public health and human lives— "green" in a different sense if you follow what we're saying.

MrBeast's video created a space to debate what is (or is not) ethical about for-profit philanthropy—faux-lanthropy, if you will—and the morality of YouTubers. It could have done what we did: talk about why the video needed to be made in the first place. The reason is that failures in the for-profit healthcare system leave behind an incredibly large number of people. There are countries around the world that make this health issue practically non-existent, but in the land of opportunity, there is a real lack of it regarding healthcare, which gives way to profitable faux-lanthropy (e.g., the work of MrBeast). Instead of recognizing healthcare as a human right, we will continue to eat the junk Jimmy Donaldson produces, and then, we will have to go to the hospital from the clogged arteries and numbed brains his "influencing" has left us with, along with a hefty tab. Jimmy, we smell another video opportunity coming . . . help a future patient out!

More recently, Donaldson ended up being defended by Elon Musk, whom readers may recall from last year's Junk Food News chapter as one of our featured billionaire dicks in space. Musk came running (or perhaps fast walking after an Ozempic episode) to the aid of MrBeast for his faux-lanthropy video about the hearing impaired. This time Beast "helped" deaf people hear for the first time—not to be confused with when he cured blindness—and was even able to do it in just six minutes! These audio-enhancing devices presented in Beast's post take time to adjust and only create the sensation of hearing, with neither of these facts noted in the video itself.[10] There were multiple opinion pieces written by deaf people criticizing this so-called healthcare video, some even referred to it as "inspiration porn," but rest assured, MrBeast's dependable fanbase and heir to apartheid emerald mine Elon, made sure to protect Donaldson and his "good deed."[11] Maybe there will be a collaboration between Mr. Musk and MrBeast soon—prosthetic dick fittings in space, perhaps? Now, *that's* what we call space junk.

THE TRUTH IS OUT THERE: SPY BALLOONS, UFOS, AND DERAILED NARRATIVES

As MrBeast cured blindness on YouTube, the Norfolk Southern Corporation hard launched the next environmental catastrophe in East Palestine, Ohio. That is so not "going green," by the way. While 1.6 million pounds of hazardous materials were being released into the town's air and water supply, causing a mass evacuation after a preventable safety issue resulted in a massive train derailment, the establishment press prioritized more pressing matters: Chinese spy balloons and potential UFOs. For nearly three days, major corporate media outlets mostly ignored the derailment while covering numerous stories about the looming "threat" of Chinese spy balloons and other unidentified flying objects. Even though US officials admitted the balloon was not a threat, corporate news outlets, including Fox, CNN, and MSNBC, continued operating under the assumption that it was.[12] From February to March, these outlets published weekly stories about the balloon to cook up a heaping pot of anti-Chinese paranoia. To ensure the safety of the American people, two brave F-22 fighter jet pilots shot down the scary blimp with a $500,000 missile—a steal in YouTube sponsorship and subscriber payout numbers.

To ensure the safety of their next budget increase, the Department of Defense broadened its paranoia campaign to potential enemies outside of the stratosphere. Coupled with the spy balloon claims were numerous reports of UFO sightings across the globe.[13] Three of these were shot down by American F-22 fighter jets, which collectively cost US taxpayers a whopping $1.6 million.[14] A fourth of this budget was wasted after one pilot failed to hit the giant object, but you can't put a price on security! The point is not to dismiss the threat of spying operations. Spying is a violation, whether it's by the United States, China, or any other country. However, the corporate media's sensationalizing of UFOs and spy balloons distracted from a much more pressing matter down here on earth: Not just the East Palestine disaster but the fact that there are roughly a thousand train derailments a year in the US.[15]

While the military played target practice and corporate media outlets went feral for anti-China headlines, the victims of East Palestine were unknowingly breathing in harmful vinyl chloride. The Norfolk Southern derailment took place on February 3, after a train's wheel bearing became so overheated that it failed.[16] It was also discovered that the trains involved did not have electronically-controlled pneumatic brakes (ECP). These are something rail worker unions have been fighting to get for many years, as ECP brakes have been instrumental in improving the safety and performance of trains.[17]

One element that the corporate press neglected in their reporting was the railway industry's successful lobbying attempts to block stronger safety regulations for trains carrying hazardous vinyl chloride. According to an article from The Lever, the Federal Railroad Administration (FRA) has known about the risks of transporting vinyl chloride by rail since the 1970s, yet the agency has failed to implement stronger safety regulations.[18] At the same time, the rail industry has lobbied against proposals to enact stronger safety measures and regulations for transporting hazardous materials, including vinyl chloride.

These proposals followed yet another Ohio derailment that occurred in 2019. Like the East Palestine derailment, the incident involved a train carrying hazardous vinyl chloride, which leaked into a nearby river. The effects led to the evacuation of thousands of nearby residents and caused significant environmental damage. Additionally, both incidents were a consequence of railroad companies cutting corners to maintain their profits. Who knew that this, paired with lifting safety regulations, would result in increased accidents? Maybe the railway unions were on to something—at least until President "Union Joe" Biden intervened, signing a bill to block a looming railway strike, partly over safety issues and paid sick days.[19]

Unlike China's so-called spy balloons and UFO sightings, the East Palestine, "Anytown, USA" story works against the corporate media's bottom line. Apparently, "MEGA CORPORATION SPARKS NEXT ENVIRONMENTAL CATASTROPHE" isn't as clickable as "CHINA LAUNCHES WORLD WAR III WITH GIANT SPY BALLOON"—just ask Joe Rogan.[20] The East Palestine story could expose the questionable actions of Norfolk Southern, a corporation that gives millions of dollars annually to anti-regulatory lobbying efforts.[21] One lobbyist, David Urban, who is also employed by CNN as a commentator, participated in a round-table discussion at the network with no mention of his relationship to Norfolk Southern.[22] Urban currently works as managing director of BGR, a lobbying group that continues to fight against transportation safety regulations. Instead of disclosing his connection with the railway company lobby group, he was identified only as a CNN commentator and former Trump campaign advisor. Dana Bash, who hosted the roundtable, did not push back when Urban attempted to shift blame away from Norfolk Southern. Urban stated: "There's plenty of blame to go around on this, on these kind—when these kinds of things happen. But what's important is what we do moving forward, right, to take care of the people in these towns and communities."

Corporate media outlets seem more interested in derailing the narrative and keeping cozy relations with PR spin doctors rather than exposing conflicts of interest or corruption. The truth is out there, but they don't seem to be interested in it.

Further, in the context of espionage and national security risks, we know, according to Pentagon sources, that the "spy" balloon (what China called a "civilian weather balloon") did not gather sensitive information from its flight over military sites, making it a much less important event than what was transpiring on a Minecraft Discord server around the same time.[23] For those who don't know, Minecraft is a video game, and Discord is a chat app that allows gamers to communicate while gaming on servers. Over the course of a month in a Minecraft Discord server, crucially sensitive information from the Pentagon was being leaked by an anonymous user (identified as 21-year-old Massachusetts Air National Guard member, Jack Teixeira) who at times would post classified info saying, "Here, have some leaked documents."[24]

It took the Pentagon a month to realize a breach had even happened, and by then, top-secret information regarding Ukraine and other military and foreign policy matters had been leaked onto the server. While the Pentagon was looking up at a balloon, they should have been looking right under their noses. Minecraft-playing teens were learning far more about statecraft than any regular block-building game would ever teach them.

MARCH *MURDER* MADNESS: FOULING OUT OFF THE COURT

Life in the twenty-first century has been anything but predictable. From the rumors of Y2K and the events of September 11 to the Great Recession and the global COVID-19 pandemic, Americans have experienced a wide range of uncertainties over the past twenty-three years. Despite this, there is one thing we can consistently rely on for excitement, drama, and general entertainment purposes—no, not MrBeast curing blindness or the media's obsession with Chinese Spy Balloons—but the wide world of sports! Yes, that's right—from the largest (and possibly the most monopolistic) non-profit to ever exist, the National Football League, to collegiate headlines and even little league T-ball, Americans never shy away from indulging in junk food sports news. Why else would ESPN report non-stop, 24/7?

It's the drama on—and *off*—the fields and courts that keeps us hooked. Athletes of all levels, professional and not, captivate audiences far beyond game day, with their personal lives, families, and extracurricular activities (legal and otherwise). This is a key example of reusing junk news: While the names change, the storylines, unfortunately, do not. Just ask OJ Simpson . . . too soon?[25] But, let's jump to the present. We all remember when the GOAT (Greatest of All Time) NFL Quarterback Tom Brady retired for fewer than forty days following the 2021 NFL season, only to abandon his family and return to the gridiron as quickly as possible in 2022. To be green and reuse his headlines, Brady has since re-announced his retirement for real this time. Also during this time, he was dumped by his world-renowned supermodel wife, adopted a kitten for his daughter, and posted viral "thirst traps" on social media. Oh, how the mighty have fallen. In more recent Brady news, he invested as a minority owner in the newly (once again) relocated and repurposed Oakland, now Las Vegas, Raiders—let's see if this fiscal move can help the Raiders live up to the adage, "What happens in Vegas, stays in Vegas."

Like the late-night infomercials always promise—*But wait, there's more!* Let's move from football to basketball. Many are familiar with NBA star Ja Morant, 23, of the Memphis Grizzlies, who was slapped with an eight-game, unpaid suspension from the league near the end of the regular 2022-2023 season. Morant's suspension followed three separate accusations of the Memphis guard's associations with potential gun violence, including an Instagram live video showing Morant flash a gun in a Denver area strip club.[26] Morant's eight-game suspension cost him nearly $700,000 of his NBA salary as he violated league policies. A flagrant 1, if you will. But our man Ja has really outdone himself when it comes to recycling junk headlines as of late. In fact, following his initial slap on the wrist from the NBA, Morant posted yet *another* Instagram live video of him flashing a gun in a car only two months later! His own team suspended him, despite being in the off-season, just months before his max contract was set to begin. What *Ja* doing, man?! When we said reuse and recycle, this is not what we meant!

But Morant is not the only basketball player connected to potential gun violence this season. NCAA

Men's Basketball has been the most unpredictable of all the sports headlines recently, busting brackets and shocking the country, upset after upset, and not just in "March Madness." In the months leading up to the collegiate basketball playoffs, Alabama Crimson Tide small forward Darius Miles and standout freshman forward Brandon Miller took part in pre-March *Murder* Madness. On January 15, 2023, a fatal shooting resulted in the death of 23-year-old mother, Jamea Harris.[27] Alabama standout Brandon Miller was accused by police of potentially supplying now-former teammate Darius Miles with the gun that was used by another man in the crime and allegedly transported the group to and from the murder of Harris.[28] Miles was arrested and removed from the team immediately, but rising collegiate star Miller remained in Alabama's starting five lineup. He is projected to be drafted into the NBA as high as the number two overall pick in June.[29] With this, Miller will likely be rewarded with a multi-million-dollar professional contract yet faces no accountability for his potential involvement in the January 15 murder—not even on his NBA draft stock value. Meanwhile, a family mourns the loss of their daughter, sister, mother, and friend.

How is it that gun violence off the court is met with acceptance if the perpetrator is good at handling a basketball? While the celebrity treatment and multi-million-dollar contracts Morant, Miller, and other professional athletes receive are unfathomable enough, the most unbelievable aspect is the leeway star players are given in cases of domestic abuse and other forms of violence.

These examples are not isolated incidents. Famous cases, like OJ Simpson, Kobe Bryant, and Ray Rice made headlines and filled the airwaves with stories of their past wrongdoings. Yet, these are just the spoiled cream of the Junk Food crop, as the media's focus is often on the players and the drama, not on the crimes. Further, when violence involving professional athletes is documented, the focus is rarely on the actual victims. Few understand the severity that the late Nicole Brown Simpson, Ron Goldman, Jamea Harris, their families, and others have faced in these circumstances. They leave behind loved ones, children, and bright futures, and their abusers often face few repercussions. In addition, when reported on, these headlines fade, and the details of the stories eventually are forgotten, but not the hype. In fact, on occasion, the corporate media actually *defend* these violent athletes, noting that their work is *meant to be* masculine, violent, and aggressive. How can Americans continue to support this junkyard of violent individuals and reward them with fame, fortune, and consistent publicity? It is time to shift the attention away from these distracting aspects of sports and focus on truly holding individuals accountable for their actions off the field and court, despite what position they play or how much money they make.

Domestic abuse and violence will only continue in public and private spheres until the media raise awareness and the punishments match the crimes. When athletes, professional and not, are accessories to manslaughter, yet are celebrated in the limelight, patterns will persist. Like how history and junk food news continue to reuse storylines, this issue will not change without the serious effort of league leadership and players, as well as fans who demand better from all of them.

ALL THE CELEBRITY JUNK WE COULDN'T THROW AWAY—SO HERE IS A SUPERSIZED BUFFET

If the decades of Junk Food News leading up to this year's publication have proven anything, it is that celebrity foibles and gossip are gifts that keep on giving. And these people truly know how to follow a script. Repeat offenders, like rapper/stalker Kanye West (aka Ye) and others, have combined to recycle their own headlines of the past. Just like how drive-thru menus get bigger boards to fit all the food items, this chapter is bursting at the seams, requiring us to puncture a new hole in our metaphorical belts. With so much junk and so little time, we realized the only option left was to curate a buffet-style montage of the celebrity Junk Food News we could not write about at length. So, prepare your stomach (and mind) to overindulge in a feast of celebrity headlines guaranteed to ruin your appetite, waistline, and critical thinking skills.

Junk Food News frequent flier, Kanye West (Ye), did not skimp out this year. We all remember him from the *Kimyé* divorce of the century last year, where he escaped the grasp of the Kardashian junkhold. Ye made himself known again this year—this time as a raging antisemite, claiming that he would go "death con 3" on Jewish people, then arguing that he, himself, could not be antisemitic because Black people were really "Jew[s]." It looked like Ye started the year on a high note when he got married to his employee Bianca Censori in January—if you don't know who she is, that's fine, we didn't either. Apparently, apart from being Ye's new girl, Censori is an Australian architect who works for Ye's brand, "Yeezy." Unfortunately for Ye, it's unlikely he'll be able to meet his new in-laws since Australia is already planning to ban him from ever entering the country. As it turns out, Australia has a history of refusing entry to known antisemitic folks and has reportedly already denied him a visa.[30] There are still countries that think praising Adolf Hitler is a bad thing—who would have thought? Although, we do need to send our regards to Jonah Hill, seeing as his decade-old movie *21 Jump Street* made Ye "like Jewish people again," causing him to post on Instagram: "Thank you Jonah Hill I love you." Apparently, an undercover cop movie starring an average Jewish guy can cure antisemitism better than basic human decency, numerous advocacy groups, or laws.

Here's the bigger problem: Ye consistently receives attention for his actions, despite the vile values they showcase. Meanwhile, little media coverage has noted that antisemitism is still a huge issue in the United States. In fact, on June 6, 2023, a judge dismissed trespassing complaints against White nationalists who prosecutors say displayed "Keep New England White" banners without a permit from an overpass in July 2022.[31] These racist banners hoisted by a neo-Nazi group appeared in New Hampshire, an original American colony that has turned blue in every presidential election since 1992, proving that racism and antisemitism are issues not just in Ye's home, but across the country, even in blue New England.[32]

Among other highly public celebrity struggles is the never-ending journey to lose weight and stay small for the camera. Stars like Mindy Kaling and Chelsea Handler started using Ozempic to shed those pesky extra pounds.[33] While the drug can be used for weight loss, it is meant for extreme cases of obesity and controlling blood sugar levels of type 2 diabetes patients. When Handler found out that

Ozempic was used by diabetics, she claimed she stopped using it; this might be one of the few times Handler willingly gave up a drug on her own accord.

Due to celebrities using Ozempic for weight loss (and therefore influencing everyday people to want it for the same reason), those with diabetes began having difficulty obtaining their supplies as the product started moving toward celebrity dieters. Some pharmacies stopped carrying the drug altogether because they were losing money since many people receiving it for weight loss had insurance, and diabetics were largely paying out of pocket.[34] Wonder what MrBeast would have to say about this? As it turns out, celebrities contributing to the for-profit healthcare market is no new phenomenon; they pretty much single-handedly created the modern plastic surgery empire! Maybe if celebs want to lose extra weight, they should drive themselves to the gym and leave the medications to the people who really need them.

Celebrity status has a way of creating a hydra of a news story, and the one born out of actress-turned-wellness guru Gwyneth "Goop" Paltrow's 2016 skiing accident grew six or seven heads this year with a televised civil court case against the actress. For those unfamiliar, retired optometrist Terry Sanderson slapped actress Gwyneth Paltrow with a lawsuit regarding an incident from 2016 in which he claimed Paltrow had collided with him while skiing in swank Park City, Utah, resulting in permanent brain damage. That is so not what shredding the pow is about, by the way. When Paltrow countersued Sanderson, out poured stories from CNN, FOX, CBS, and NBC on every second of the eight-day court proceeding. All the major outlets covered daily details of the trial. Fox even doubled up on their coverage on a few occasions.[35] Well, Sanderson lost, but after Paltrow's paltry $1 payout and memories of the trial melting away, CBS, Fox, and even the *Guardian* saw mountains of opportunity left in "news stories" about the plaintiff's fame-hunger, legal bills, internet regrets, and remaining legal options.[36] From a corporate media perspective, that one 2016 ski collision was the 2023 Goop gift that kept giving. We get it: An embarrassingly large number of people (an estimated 30 million) watched some portion of the trial, likely taking a toll on their wellness, which corporate media discovered resulted in an uptick in clickety-clicks online (cha-ching!).[37]

Meanwhile, non-profit, independent news outlet Grist directed attention to Utah for another reason: the passage of a state law that created stricter consequences for protesting at pipeline construction sites and other "critical infrastructure sites," cracking down on Americans' civil liberties. Rooted in climate journalism, Grist saw cause to publicize this story because the Utah legislation's verbiage will likely impact peaceful environmental protestors, especially since prison sentences could now reflect felony charges.[38] As it turns out, in Utah, you have a higher chance of the government eroding your First Amendment rights than getting lit up on the slopes by an uppity celeb. Corporate media sources like the *New York Times*, CNN, and HuffPost all published one-off stories in years past mentioning the states that approved similar laws in the wake of the Dakota Access pipeline protests. But, given the coin in airing a universally-hated celebrity getting sued by an even more unlikeable geezer, these outlets were unsurprisingly quiet about this environmental news out of Utah. Can't upset the fossil fuel daddies, their loyal lobbyists, and politician simps, eh? Corporate wellness really is the bottom line.

CONCLUSION

So, as it turns out, celebrity Junk Food News tastes just as good served buffet style. We did our best to go green this year as headlines from the past found themselves in the mainstream once again. And in an effort to reduce the waste of future Junk Food News, we'll have to get a scrap bucket to repurpose for next year's chapter.

Anyhow, why would Americans focus on things that actually matter when they can tune into MrBeast's faux-lanthropy on YouTube or big Chinese spy balloons and UFOs that fill the sky? Caring about serious stories that often do not appear on corporate news outlets could lead to a more well-rounded, better-educated society. But who would want that? Certainly not those in the for-profit health care system, greedy corporate executives and their lobbyists, ultra-rich athletes and celebrities, or any other power-wielding talking heads in the establishment press. The sad truth is that Americans love their Junk Food News. Without such distractions and junk news vices, we risk facing reality—or worse . . . thinking critically? We all do our patriotic duty keeping the distractions alive, gorging ourselves at the buffet of Junk Food News. Because Ozempic will take care of the rest, right?

Wrong. It is up to us, the consumers of news, to inspire a shift in the media landscape. We as a society must recognize that none of these stories offer groundbreaking or revolutionary insights. The goal of Junk Food News is to distract audiences from what's important. If consumers spend their days feasting on the spam of cultural commentary and celebrity hit pieces, how can they make room for substantive news, the stories that have a *meaningful* impact on our lives? We may never understand life as a Kardashian, but the average person may endure the failures of American healthcare, the cost of climate disasters, the horrific reality of domestic abuse and violence, or the loss of civil liberties. We can, and must, demand better from our Fourth Estate, replacing empty calorie stories with nutritious news we can use. Our health as a nation depends on it.

JEN LYONS is an instructor of history for several college campuses throughout the San Francisco Bay Area and Northern Nevada. Lyons earned both her BA and MA in history from the University of Nevada, Reno. She spends her free time stressing out over the Las Vegas Raiders and other professional sports teams. She currently resides in Denver, CO.

SIERRA KAUL is a recent UC Davis graduate who majored in history. She plans on receiving a graduate degree in Library Sciences, and if that doesn't work out, she plans on screaming into the void as a job. Her lifelong goal is to one day stay at the haunted Clown Motel in Tonopah, Nevada.

REAGAN HAYNIE is a 2023 graduate from Loyola Marymount with a degree in Communication Studies. Her interests include anti-imperialist journalism, vintage skirts, niche perfumes, and Chicago house music.

MARCELLE LEVINE SWINBURNE teaches California, US, and women's history at Diablo Valley College and Solano Community College. Current research interests include the history of clothing and fashion and the history of family life. In her free time, Marcelle enjoys scrapbooking and entertaining her infant son.

GAVIN KELLEY is a Cal State Long Beach graduate with a degree in creative writing. He wields his pen as an arts organization administrator and is currently director of operations for the Colburn School's dance program. A kung fu practitioner and a martial arts movie podcaster and fan, Gavin developed a keen eye for Junk Food News after years of studying straight-to-video B movies. He co-hosts the *Martial Arts Mania Podcast*.

MICKEY HUFF is director of Project Censored and president of the Media Freedom Foundation. He is also a professor of social science, history, and journalism at Diablo Valley College where he co-chairs the history area and is chair of the Journalism Department. He has co-edited and contributed to Project Censored's annual books since 2009. Junk Food News analysis has long been one of his guilty pleasures.

Notes

1   For a more detailed introduction to Junk Food News, see Carl Jensen, *Censored: The News That Didn't Make the News-and Why* (Chapel Hill, NC: Shelburne Press, 1993), 89-96.
2   MrBeast, "1,000 Blind People See for the First Time," YouTube, January 28, 2023, video, 8:00.
3   "(Popular) Videos," MrBeast, YouTube, accessed June 12, 2023.
4   Adam Fitch, "What is MrBeast's Net Worth and How Does He Make Money?" Dexerto, July 4, 2023.
5   Jimmy Donaldson (@MrBeast), "I don't understand why curable blindness is a thing. Why don't governments step in and help? Even if you're thinking purely from a financial standpoint it's hard to see how they don't roi on taxes from people being able to work again," Twitter post, January 30, 2023, 6:14 a.m.
6   "Billing and Insurance," Records & Billing, Cedars Sinai, undated [accessed July 12, 2023].
7   Elisabeth Rosenthal, "As Hospital Prices Soar, a Stitch Tops $500," *New York Times*, December 2, 2013.
8   Emily Kirk, "Operation Miracle: A New Vision of Public Health?" *International Journal of Cuban Studies* 3, no. 4 (2011): 366–81.

9   Mary Murray, "Katrina Aid from Cuba? No Thanks, Says U.S.," NBC News, September 12, 2005.

10   Liam O'Dell, "Opinion: Deaf People like Me Deserve Better than MrBeast's 'Inspiration Porn,'" Independent, May 7, 2023.

11   Reena Koh, "The YouTube Video of MrBeast Giving Hearing Aids to 1,000 Deaf People Has the Internet Divided—and Now Elon Musk Is Involved, Too," Insider, May 8, 2023.

12   Ben Norton, "US Admits Weather Pushed Chinese Balloon off Course, US Shot Down Hobbyists' $12 Balloon in $2M Missile Attack," Geopolitical Economy, February 18, 2023.

13   Derrick Bryson Taylor, "A Timeline of the U.F.O.s That Were Shot Down," New York Times, February 21, 2023.

14   Mark Moore and Caitlin Doornbos, "US Military Spent Millions to Shoot Down Three Harmless UFOs," New York Post, February 23, 2023.

15   David Sirota et al., "Over 1,000 Trains Derail Every Year in America. Let's Bring That Number Down," New York Times, February 17, 2023. See Chapter 4 of this volume for additional analysis of media coverage of the train derailment.

16   "50-Car Train Derailment Causes Big Fire, Evacuations in Ohio," AP News, February 4, 2023.

17   National Transportation Safety Board, "Norfolk Southern Railway Train Derailment with Subsequent Hazardous Material Release and Fires," NTSB, March 21, 2023.

18   David Sirota et al., "Rail Companies Blocked Safety Rules Before Ohio Derailment," The Lever, February 8, 2023.

19   Philip Elliot, "Why 'Union Joe' Chose to Make it Illegal for Rail Workers to Strike," Time, December 2, 2022.

20   JRE Forever (@jre_4ever), "Joe Rogan talks with Krystal Ball and Saagar Enjeti about the chinese spy balloon . . . ," TikTok, February 4, 2023.

21   Justin Sweitzer, "Norfolk Southern Has Spent Millions on Lobbying and Political Donations. Will It Pay Off?" City & State PA, April 3, 2023.

22   Eric Hananoki, "CNN Commentator Lobbied for Norfolk Southern; the Network Didn't Tell Its Audience during East Palestine Discussion," Media Matters for America, February 27, 2023.

23   Chloe Kim, "Chinese Spy Balloon Did Not Collect Information, Says Pentagon," BBC, June 30, 2023; Courtney Kube and Carol E. Lee, "Chinese Spy Balloon Gathered Intelligence from Sensitive U.S. Military Sites, Despite U.S. Efforts to Block It," NBCNews, April 3, 2023.

24   Matthew Loh, "Leaked Pentagon Documents Appeared on a 'Minecraft' Discord Server Weeks before Officials Knew about a Breach: Report," Insider, April 12, 2023.

25   See the reference to OJ Simpson in the Junk Food News chapter in Carl Jensen, Project Censored, 20 Years of Censored News (New York: Seven Stories Press, 1994).

26   Tim Reynolds, "NBA Suspends Ja Morant 8 Games for Video Showing Gun in Club," Associated Press, March 15, 2023.

27   Nicole Acosta, "Star Alabama Basketball Player Accused of Providing Gun Used in Killing of Woman," People, February 22, 2023.

28   Acosta, "Star Alabama Basketball Player."

29   Kyle Boone, "Sixteen Top NBA Draft Prospects in the Sweet 16: Alabama's Brandon Miller, Arkansas' Nick Smith Look Strong," CBS, March 22, 2023.

30   Carly Silva, "Why Kanye West Might Be Barred from Visiting New Wife's Family in Australia," *Parade*, January 25, 2023.

31   Associated Press, "NH Judge Dismisses Trespassing Complaints over 'Keep New England White' Overpass Banners," Fox News, June 6, 2023.

32   CBS News Boston, "Charges Dismissed against Men over 'Keep New England White' Banner on NH Overpass, CBS, June 7, 2023.

33   Kaitlin Simpson, "Chelsea Handler, Kyle Richards and More Celebrities Who've Spoken About the Ozempic Weight Loss Trend," *Us Weekly*, March 6, 2023.

34   Christine Fallabel, "How People with Diabetes Are Getting by During the Ozempic Shortage," diaTribe, February 6, 2023.

35   Tracy Wright, "Gwyneth Paltrow's Ski Crash Testimony May Give Her Advantage with Jury as Legal Experts Dissect Trial," Fox News, March 28, 2023; Caroline Thayer and Lauren Overhultz, "Gwyneth Paltrow's Version of Ski Collision 'Matches' Laws of Physics: Expert," Fox News, March 28, 2023.

36   Ramon Antonio Vargas, "Suing Gwyneth Paltrow 'Absolutely Not' Worth It, Says Utah Man," *The Guardian*, April 1, 2023; Megan Cerullo, "Plaintiff Who Sued Gwyneth Paltrow Could Owe Big Bucks in Legal Fees," CBS News, April 3, 2023; Emily Trainham, "Plaintiff in Gwyneth Paltrow's Ski Crash Trial Regrets Lawsuit: 'I'm Going to Be on the Internet Forever,'" Fox News, April 1, 2023.

37   Matt Donnelly, "Gwyneth Paltrow Ski Trial: Nearly 30 Million People Watched across YouTube, Social Platforms," *Variety*, March 31, 2023.

38   Naveena Sadasivam, "Welcome to Utah, Where Pipeline Protests Could Now Get You at Least Five Years in Prison," Grist, March 21, 2023.

CHAPTER 4:

Lies, Misdirection, and Propaganda
News Abuse in Service of Elite Interests

ROBIN ANDERSEN

When George Santos ran for United States Congress in 2022 to represent New York's Third District, the 34-year-old serial liar won the seat. *The Guardian* later reported, "He has since admitted embellishing his résumé." The *embellishments* included outrageous claims, from leading the Baruch College volleyball team to victory—after which he needed two knee replacements—to graduating summa cum laude.[1] Yet he never attended CUNY's Baruch College. He then lied about producing a Spider-Man musical, and that members of his family were Holocaust victims, later having to contend that he was only "Jew-ish." In July 2021, Santos tweeted that the 9/11 attacks on the World Trade Center "claimed" his mother's life, although she died of cancer in 2016. The paper reported that all these fabrications "have been disproven," yet the *Guardian* never used the word *lied* or charged him with being a liar.[2] Only after the election, and after local demonstrators protested with signs demanding the freshman congressman resign ("Say no to Santos"), did establishment media run with the story.[3] However, a small local Long Island paper, the *North Shore Leader*, broke the scandal months earlier during the campaign.[4]

The great failure of the press to carry out the bare minimum of its journalistic mandate—to hold political figures accountable in a representative democracy, and to at least question such obvious electoral fabrications—are prime examples of what Peter Phillips, director of Project Censored from 1996-2010, identified as *News Abuse*. The complacency of corporate media is a crucial indicator of America's declining democracy, and exposing media distortions and misdirection, including the spread of corporate and government propaganda (in all its many forms, both systemic and targeted), is the mandate for the study of News Abuse. Its analysis is the starting point for understanding the ongoing toxic political environment and the dangerous discourses that have led to devastating consequences for freedom of expression and the press. In the case of George Santos, after the election, when each newly discovered lie seemed to lead to another one, corporate media never looked inward to admit their bungling of the story, and the coverage rapidly grew worse.

THE CLOWN SHOW AND LYING AS THE NEW NORMAL

As the Santos story played out in US media at the beginning of 2023, federal prosecutors levied numerous charges against the junior congressman; his charity was a heartless scam, and a former aide accused him of sexual harassment.[5] His history of crossdressing during Carnival in Brazil was met with titillating discussions. Rather than characterizing Santos as an outrageous liar, establishment news outlets portrayed him as a disturbed buffoon. A *New York Post* headline used the word "clown," reporting that

Santos admitted to lying about graduating from Baruch College and "also copped to fibbing about working for Goldman Sachs."[6] He was gleefully credited by the *New York Times* for making the Baruch volleyball team famous, as the paper quoted the trite marketing cliché, "What do they say—any publicity is good publicity . . ."[7]

A clear example of News Abuse, this reporting trivialized George Santos's actions while burying consideration of the significant dangers to democracy of a successful electoral campaign based on lies a proactive press could easily have exposed before election day. Though some members of both parties and Long Island voters called on Santos to quit, his support of Kevin McCarthy's tortured bid to become Speaker of the House provided political protection for Santos.[8] In spring 2023, Santos announced he would run again for office in 2024, a pronouncement that sparked another round of news coverage focused on memes and other forms of commentary that mocked Santos.[9]

When CBS invited another dangerous far-right politician, the conspiracy theorist Marjorie Taylor Greene, onto its flagship news show *60 Minutes*, host Lesley Stahl was no match for the notorious fabricator.[10] Stahl lost the discursive battle when she asked Greene about her Facebook comment that the 2018 Parkland shooting in Florida (which left seventeen students and staff dead) was a "false flag" operation.[11] Even though *60 Minutes* showed a screenshot of Greene's now-deleted Facebook comment, Greene lied about lying.

"I never said Parkland was a false flag," Greene answered, "No, I've never said that."[12]

Stahl was unprepared for the subsequent indignant rant unleashed by Greene, whose aggressive outrage served to render her appearance on the show a positive political event.[13] Greene sits on two key congressional committees: the House Oversight Committee and the Homeland Security Committee.[14]

Donald Trump is now also given the carnivalesque ratings-draw treatment, and much of Trump news is a breathless sideshow that trivializes what should be treated with gravity and serious analysis. Once again, corporate media seemed to forget the extravagant, well-documented lies and their consequences, which the former-President has used so effectively to poison the political process.[15] When Trump was indicted on thirty-four felony counts and forced to turn himself in to New York prosecutors, much of the press focused on the crowds assembled in Florida and New York to watch the spectacle.[16] One well-known vlogger told HuffPost he showed up at the park because "it feels like the center of the universe when you see this on television." A member of the New York Young Republican Club, Paul Ingrassia, who wore a suit and "his hair slicked back," attended to show support for Trump. As a media scrum formed around now-Republican-celebrity George Santos, Ingrassia was quoted saying, "A lot of what he said isn't lies."[17] Despite the corporate media's shortcomings in reporting the Santos story, in May 2023, the Department of Justice charged him with a thirteen-count indictment that aimed to hold Santos "accountable for various alleged fraudulent schemes and brazen misrepresentations," according to Breon Peace, the United States Attorney for the Eastern District of New York.[18]

In this year's news cycle, although political discourse hinged on lies told by political candidates and elected officials with a variety of motivations, the press corps' tepid coverage yielded one common result: protection of the powerful. Big Tech censorship (supposedly to block fake news) is also undertaken with justifications that are themselves lies. Sorting out the reasons, practices, and motivations for the media ecology of lying may help us better detect lies and tell some truth about political prevarications. The mounting obfuscations of corporate news expand as it struggles to frame the world in ways that normalize the bottom-line ethos of the "free market," while obscuring the reality and consequences of systemic corporate malfeasance.

The third decade of the twenty-first century—marked by the collective threats of nuclear Armageddon, environmental collapse, and an economic future dominated by the power of a wealthy few—is an age marred by the merger between government, corporate power, and establishment media. Political analyst Sheldon Wolin observes that a "symbiotic relationship exists between traditional government and the system of private governance represented by modern business corporations." This merger has led to what the author calls "inverted totalitarianism," referring to a system that represents "the political coming of age of corporate power."[19]

The best illustration of the age of corporate power is the long genesis of the Ohio train derailment and the disaster it created. Years of collusion between the government and the rail industry, termed "regulatory capture" by Mickey Huff, and uncritical media coverage, led to an environmental emergency perpetrated by a for-profit corporation against a large swath of the American homeland.[20] An examination of the themes and strategies journalists employed to report the disaster, including what was said and what was excluded as the story developed, reveals a solid commitment to the ethos of corporate power. Concern for human well-being, basic fairness for workers, or care for the earth's ecosystem and the life it supports does not factor into the narrative themes of corporate media. From sensationalistic formats that draw ratings, to media consolidation, commercialization, and affiliate marketing, we live in an age of full-blown monetized news media at every level.[21] The de facto biases built into this corporatized system, which have been developing for decades, emerged full-blown at the scene of the devastating train disaster.

THE OHIO TRAIN DISASTER: FAILURES OF GOVERNMENT OVERSIGHT AND CORPORATE MEDIA

On February 3, 2023, an eastbound Norfolk Southern freight train carrying 150 cars, including at least five tanker cars containing vinyl chloride, a Class 2 flammable gas and known carcinogen, derailed in East Palestine, Ohio, close to the Pennsylvania border. Because of industry lobbying, the train had been exempted from the "high-hazard flammable train" classification that requires more stringent safety regulations.[22] In the following days, vinyl chloride and other unknown toxic chemicals would be released into the atmosphere, exacerbated by a "controlled burn" that lasted for days. The spill would kill wildlife and fish for miles, as residents complained of toxic air quality that burned their eyes and made it hard to breathe. Though EPA officials announced that the community's water was safe to drink, it was subsequently revealed that sloppy, inaccurate water testing was conducted by the rail industry itself.[23]

Images of the environmental and public health catastrophe published by NOAA's Air Resources Laboratory used atmospheric transport and dispersion models known as HYSPLIT to track cancer-causing air particles as far north as Montreal, Canada.[24] Corporate media reported what could be seen on the ground with images of the black cloud of smoke looming over the landscape, nearly indistinguishable from the cinematography of disaster films. Overhead shots of the piled-up train cars, jammed accordion-style, dominated coverage. Following sensationalized visual footage, the disaster frame focused corporate media toward official announcements and reactions, offering little in the way of background context. That was left to independent news sources.

For example, The Lever published a timely and impressive body of work that detailed years of corporate lobbying and government compliance (under various administrations) aimed at undermining regulatory oversight.[25] Safety measures across the rail industry had been effectively blocked for years, leaving in place a Civil War-era braking system, no requirement to identify many toxic chemicals, and a lack of steel-lined rail cars capable of containing chemicals after a train derailment, among others.[26] Rail companies, including Norfolk Southern, claimed that added safety measures were too expensive, and they continued to increase the number of cars per train, even as they laid off thousands of workers and delivered billions of dollars in profits to CEOs and shareholders.[27]

An extensive content analysis of network news reporting between February 4 and February 13 demonstrated the degree to which corporate media failed to inform the American public about the causes and context of the derailment. Media Matters for America found that major TV news networks on cable (CNN, Fox News Channel, and MSNBC) and broadcast (ABC, CBS, and NBC) aired nearly three hours of coverage on the Ohio train derailment, across ninety-two segments, but only two programs, both airing on February 13, addressed "how regulations governing the transport of hazardous materials by rail were weakened under multiple administrations by rail industry lobbyists, including those representing Norfolk Southern." The study concluded that national TV news "failed to incorporate critical context about the rail industry's efforts to weaken safety regulations."[28]

While avoiding the long history of scuttled regulatory oversight, corporate news found other angles and stories. For one Bloomberg writer, the biggest problem of the train derailment was not the environmental disaster itself but the "bungled messaging." The writer also complained of too many "rumors of dead chickens."[29] As social media, and especially Twitter, amplified reporting by The Lever and other independent sources, some Washington lawmakers and Biden administration officials began to consider tougher regulations on trains carrying hazardous materials.[30] Troubled by the possibility of a new regulatory push, the rail industry doubled down on a propaganda blitz, buying space in Politico's "Huddle" newsletter for messages produced by PR crisis management teams and formatted to look like native content, alleging the industry's commitment to safety.

The Establishment Press as Purveyors of Corporate Propaganda

The Lever identified Politico as a "Beltway news outlet" that helped popularize the "native advertising" model where lobbyists spin the news affecting their members' industries. The dynamics of "market journalism" and the withholding of content critical of corporate clients have long been understood. During past regulatory battles, rail lobbyists relied on prominent news outlets—including the *New York Times*, *Washington Post*, and Vox—to print their preferred narratives in the form of ads designed to look like legitimate news articles.[31] After the derailment, the *New York Times* also ran interference for the industry, downplaying the severity of the environmental consequences by reporting, "For many influencers across the political spectrum, claims about the environmental effects of the train derailment have gone far beyond known facts." But compared to previous PR published under the banner of the *New York Times*, that sounded like real reporting. In one advertorial published by the *Times*, the fantastical text declared, "The industry's investments in technology have made freight rail a pillar of the U.S. economy and the world's model of safety, sustainability and efficiency."[32] In 2015, as the rail industry was fighting to block an Obama-era rule that would have required electronic braking technology on some hazmat trains, Vox published an ad from the Association of American Railroads proclaiming the rail industry's "relentless approach to safety—one in which good is never good enough."[33]

In reality, corporate profits pushing larger trains, smaller staff sizes, and more cost-cutting measures have resulted in more than one thousand train derailments across the US each year.[34] In a piece for the Real News Network, titled "This Was Preventable," railroad workers explained how Wall Street caused the East Palestine derailment. The Real News Network's Maximillian Alvarez talked to Jeff Kurtz and Mark Burrows of Railroad Workers United, who explained "how corporate greed has destroyed our supply chain and put our communities at perpetual risk of derailments like this."[35] In fall 2022, as lawmakers were voting to bust a looming strike and impose a labor contract on rail workers with no provision for paid sick time, the Association of American Railroads ran ads in Politico claiming the contract "charts a better, stronger future for our employees and industry, and the economy."[36] Instead of providing the public with essential information, major media outlets allowed industry to buy and promote propaganda under their legitimatizing banners. When critical information about sponsoring industries is muted, the escalating monetization of corporate news degrades journalism. Mickey Huff confirmed in an interview on the *Ralph Nader Radio Hour* that the Norfolk Southern crash was "a bipartisan disaster ... and it shows, once again, the gross failure of the corporate media."[37]

Once independent news outlets, including The Lever and the Intercept, exposed the industry practices and lax government regulation that led to this preventable disaster, corporate media could no longer ignore the story, and politicians could no longer refuse to act.[38] But that type of critical reporting is not without its dangers.

Dangers to Journalists, Activists, and Environmental Defenders Who Bear Witness

At a press conference held by Ohio Governor Mike DeWine on February 9, 2023, Evan Lambert, a correspondent for NewsNation, finished his live report about the train derailment as law enforcement officers told him to leave the elementary school auditorium where the briefing was being held. As documented in a video posted by the Associated Press, police officers subsequently surrounded Lambert, pushed him to the ground, and handcuffed him.[39] Images showed Lambert being held face down on a concrete floor and hauled away with his hands cuffed behind his back. George Washington University journalism professor Frank Sesno said he was "very disturbed" by the physical force being used on Lambert.[40] Lambert was charged for doing the work of journalism. The Committee to Protect Journalists promptly called on law enforcement in East Palestine to drop the official charges of disorderly conduct and criminal trespass, which it eventually did.[41]

The most egregious attacks on journalists globally are designed to silence those who bear witness by exposing the most extreme crimes of war, planetary destruction, and global human rights violations. WikiLeaks publisher Julian Assange has been detained in the UK's Belmarsh high security prison since April 11, 2019, an imprisonment that totals twelve years of arbitrary detention identified as torture by the UN Special Rapporteur on Torture, Nils Melzer.[42] Assange is fighting extradition to the United States where he has been indicted for crimes of espionage for publishing truthful information in the public interest and exposing US war crimes in Iraq.[43] If the US prosecution of Assange is successful, it will set a legal precedent with extreme chilling effects for all journalists and publishers.[44] The executive director of the Freedom of the Press Foundation, Trevor Timm, explained that the continuing push to prosecute Assange using the Espionage Act is a betrayal of the journalistic principles the Biden administration has taken credit for celebrating. Timm added that this kind of abuse of the Espionage Act against sources—and now journalists and publishers—"is an embarrassment to basic ideals of justice and to core First Amendment values."[45] Additional organizations including the American Civil Liberties Union, Reporters Without Borders, Human Rights Watch, and the Committee to Protect Journalists have joined the Freedom of the Press Foundation to fight the prosecution of Julian Assange. In addition, the editors and publishers of leading newspapers have called for charges against Assange to be dropped, even though Western media sources have demonized Assange over the years.[46] As Eve Ottenberg noted the "media mockery" of Assange "turned out to be entirely wrong."[47] US lawmakers have called on attorney general Merrick Garland to stop the prosecution of Assange.[48] Yet Washington continues its egregious persecution of him, working to criminalize journalism, even as it claims "journalism is not a crime."[49]

THE FIRST ANNIVERSARY OF THE WAR IN UKRAINE: ALL WAR ALL THE TIME

Many factors have led to a pro-war, pro-Western consensus in establishment journalism as independent views are suppressed and the people who express them are treated with ridicule and contempt.[50] Policy positions that argue against belligerencies in favor of negotiations are all but absent from news cycles.[51] Media critics have identified a pro-Western bias in press coverage of Ukraine, which constitutes one of the most notable cases of News Abuse this year.[52] As Bryce Greene pointed out, the roots of the escalations leading up to the war in Ukraine were "completely omitted from the Western media."[53] When corporate media did "explain" the war in Ukraine, it "almost universally gave a pro-Western view of US/Russia relations."[54] Meanwhile troves of documents and investigations about the extent of Western propaganda and anti-Russian information management campaigns have recently been published across a range of online media.[55] However, as with most wars, opinion polls showed slacking public support for US involvement in the war while the conflict in Ukraine continued with no resolution in sight. For example, in spring 2023, 59 percent of the US public said that limiting damage to the US economy was more important than sanctioning Russia. The *PBS NewsHour* reported that, in March 2022, "the situation was reversed: 55 percent said it was a bigger priority to sanction Russia effectively, even if it meant damage to the US economy."[56] Yet Pentagon spending is rarely tied to damage done to the US domestic economy.

The first anniversary of the devastating war in Ukraine was memorialized with stories of bravery and determination and the strong "Biden-Zelensky bond," taking up the front page of the *New York Times* above the fold, with more photographs taken over the course of the war featured on the paper's inside pages.[57] Few scenes of the horrors of war or accounts of the need to negotiate the conflict between two super powers were evident in media coverage. Such war propaganda has far-reaching consequences and has led to the most "wildly overfunded military on the planet," even though the US military has not won a significant conflict since the second world war.[58] As Tom Engelhardt asserted, from Vietnam to Afghanistan, nothing has stopped the US military from being "massively overfunded by whatever administration is in power or whatever party controls Congress." There is no significant skepticism in political discourse as "the one-party state in this country...remains the Pentagon."[59] The severity of the lockdown on public debate about the war in Ukraine was illustrated when a letter from thirty progressive politicians to President Biden, advocating negotiations to end the war, was withdrawn the very the next day because of "blowback."[60]

The Pentagon also has enormous influence in shaping popular culture and promoting narratives of militarism across the media spectrum. Since the second half of the twentieth century, the power of the Pentagon over films and entertainment has permeated Hollywood, resulting in a near complete lack of critical narratives, as detailed by filmmaker Roger Stahl's documentary *Theaters of War*, which screened at film festivals, on university campuses, and online in 2022.[61] The media consensus that reinforces a militarized ethos of belligerencies over any other solution to conflict attests to the intensity of war propaganda, as its influence extends from Hollywood to the reporting of war itself.

THE NORD STREAM PIPELINES, THE US MILITARY, AND CORPORATE MEDIA

Reporting for MintPress News, Jonathan Cook characterized the September 2022 destruction of the Nord Stream pipelines as "an act of unrivaled industrial and environmental terrorism." "Someone blew up the Nord Stream pipelines," he wrote, "creating an untold environmental catastrophe as the pipes leaked huge quantities of methane, a supremely active global-warming gas."[62] The Nord Stream pipelines were a multibillion-dollar infrastructure project built by Russia to deliver cheap natural gas to Europe along the seafloor of international waters in the Baltic Sea. Three of the four pipelines were blown up on September 27, 2022. For almost two weeks, the claim that Russia was responsible for the sabotage made the rounds on the headlines of Western news outlets. Much of US media, from Bloomberg to cable news, pointed to Russian culpability.[63] *The Washington Post* reported, "European Leaders Blame Russian 'Sabotage' After Nord Stream Explosions," citing European Union officials who admitted they had no evidence of Russian involvement but asserted that Russia had the means and the "motivation."[64] However, the implausible explanation seemed to raise more questions than it answered.

The news frame of Russian responsibility was difficult to maintain, partly because gas and oil revenues financed nearly half of the nation's annual budget. In addition to causing Russia great financial harm, the blasts also diminished Moscow's influence over Germany, which had been heavily dependent on Russian gas. As MintPress News noted, the narrative required Western publics to believe

"President Vladimir Putin willingly shot himself in the foot, losing his only leverage over European resolve to impose economic sanctions on his country."[65] Yet the country with the greatest motivation, the one that had already threatened the pipelines, was the United States.

Writing for Fairness & Accuracy in Reporting (FAIR), Bryce Greene pointed to well-established, longstanding opposition to the pipeline by US officials as evidence of Washington's motivation. More specifically, in February 2022, the Associated Press reported that President Joe Biden "has threatened to block the Nord Stream 2 natural gas pipeline if Russia invades Ukraine."[66] After the blasts, Biden's past proclamations flew across the internet on numerous social media platforms. Later, the video of top US diplomat Victoria Nuland celebrating the Nord Stream bombing at a Senate hearing would also make the rounds. Nuland said, "I think the administration is very gratified to know that Nord Stream 2 is now . . . a hunk of metal at the bottom of the sea."[67] As Greene stated, "most newsrooms uniformly suppressed this history, and attacked those who raised it."[68] When some journalists recalled the White House statement and fingered the United States as a possible culprit, establishment media labeled their assertions "fake news." As a subsequent Associated Press report asserted, without evaluating any evidence, the idea that the United States was responsible for the blasts was a "conspiracy theory" and "disinformation" designed to "undermine Ukraine's allies."[69] According to AP's report, the suggestion that the United States "caused the damage was circulating on online forums popular with American conservatives and followers of QAnon, a conspiracy theory movement which asserts that Trump is fighting a battle against a Satanic child-trafficking sect that controls world events." The AP report was picked up by numerous US press outlets. No mention was made to the legitimate alternative and independent journalists, bloggers, and social media users who were also challenging Western assertions of Russian culpability.

In a piece titled "It's Only a 'Conspiracy Theory' When It Accuses the US Government," Caitlin Johnstone exposed the double standard embedded in establishment press coverage of Nord Stream 2: "If you think the United States could have any responsibility for this attack at all, you're a crazy conspiracy theorist and no different from QAnoners who think pedophile Satan worshipers rule the world."[70] Instead, Johnstone pointed out, "Over and over again we see the pejorative 'conspiracy theory' applied to accusations against one nation but not the other."

The exception to the rule appeared on Bloomberg TV when host Tom Keene interviewed Columbia University economist Jeffrey Sachs. During the interview, Sachs stated that he "would bet [the attack] was a US action, perhaps US and Poland." Among other things, Sachs cited the threatening statements by President Biden and Secretary of State Anthony Blinken, and then confronted the US media consensus by saying:

I know . . . you're not allowed to say these things in the West, but the fact of the matter is, all over the world when I talk to people, they think the US did it. . . . Even reporters on our papers that are involved tell me privately, "Of course [the US is responsible]," but it doesn't show up in our media.[71]

The interview with Sachs was pulled off the air.[72] Despite the enormity of the event, as the credibility of Russian culpability plummeted, the Nord Stream pipelines story was shelved. It disappeared from media coverage for months.[73]

That changed in February 2023 when renowned journalist Seymour Hersh—who was awarded a Pulitzer Prize for his 1970 reporting on My Lai and exposed the Abu Ghraib prisoner abuse scandal in Iraq—published his investigation into the destruction of the Nord Stream pipelines.[74] His Substack report detailed how the operation was carried out by a Florida-based team of US Navy divers with the help of the Norwegian military. The exposé was the latest in Hersh's venerable career as a journalist revered for accuracy and integrity, but instead of pursuing the leads and evidence included in Hersh's report, the establishment press ignored, discredited, or dismissed it. Many outlets quoted US military officials' statements— which simply denied Hersh's allegations—as conclusive. One Reuters headline read, "White House Says Blog Post on Nord Stream Explosion 'Utterly False'"[75] In an attempt to trivialize and distract, the *New York Times* handed its opinion page over to Ross Douthat, whose barely coherent meanderings merged the Nord Stream puzzle to questions about the origins of UFOs, whether Jeffrey Epstein killed himself, what happened between Brett Kavanaugh and Christine Blasey Ford, and other "unsolved mysteries of our time."[76]

Newsweek had a different take on the blown gas pipelines, but instead of drawing out the consequences of a US government act of terrorism or the escalation of direct US conflict with an armed nuclear power, authors John Yoo and Robert Delahunty (who have notoriously coauthored memos justifying torture) criticized President Biden for ordering the attack without congressional authorization: "For military actions far less consequential than this, Biden used to attack his Republican predecessors as 'monarchists,'" Yoo and Delahunty asserted.[77] *Newsweek* framed the Nord Stream attack primarily as a partisan battle between rival political parties over the limits of executive power.

Referring to de-platforming, content warnings, and denying access to Hersh's pipeline story, another long-time war analyst, Patrick Lawrence, invoked "the disinformation industry" and referred to what he called "diabolic organizations" posing as fact-checking entities, including PropOrNot, NewsGuard, and Hamilton 68, which are "stocked with spooks" who use their positions as staff and advisors to discredit "dissenting writers and independent publications as conveyers of Russian propaganda."[78] (Alan MacLeod of MintPress News has documented the role of ex-CIA officers in shaping Facebook's content policies and former FBI officials working for Google and Twitter.[79]) Lawrence's report confirms what we have come to understand as a major step in war propaganda—the use of Russiagate as the boogeyman, a notional discourse that must be silenced, an enemy so hideous it must be made unspeakable. It need only be evoked to delegitimize and discredit, and much worse, used as a blanket justification to remove, de-platform, and silence dissenting online speech.

THE "RUSSIAGATE" FAKE NEWS STORY

In 2022, new research emerged about Russiagate, a story that Project Censored has tracked since it identified reporting critical of Russiagate as one of its top "Censored" stories of 2017-2018.[80] The narrative took hold with claims that Russian propaganda played a major role in the 2016 election of Donald J. Trump. Though no evidence of Russia's purportedly pervasive and influential online campaign was ever published, Russiagate news was, nevertheless, a key factor in the moral panic that led to calls for content "moderation" across social media.[81] However, by 2022, academic researchers, independent journalists, and analysts confirmed the falsity of Russiagate. A New York University study of Russian Twitter campaigns found no influence on the 2016 presidential election that brought Donald Trump to power.[82] On January 30, 2023, Jeff Gerth, a Pulitzer Prize-winning journalist, began a four-part series in the *Columbia Journalism Review* documenting how doubts about the veracity of claims of Russian interference were repeatedly ignored by the establishment press in their push to hold the narrative together.[83] Yet the demands for "content moderation" to address Russian-sourced "fake news" continue apace.

With no countervailing force or establishment media argumentation to challenge the escalation of war between two nuclear powers, the threat of a third world war looms larger every day.[84] As *Jacobin* pointed out, sixty years ago we narrowly avoided a nuclear holocaust, but a review of media coverage at the time shows diplomacy was not taboo then, as it seems to be now. "Today's political establishment," Branko Marcetic wrote, "has adopted nearly word for word the rhetoric of Cold War hawks who would have killed us all."[85]

CONCLUSION

From political campaigns and environmental disasters to war and the exposure of systemic censorship, establishment media seem incapable of clarification, explanation, or even sketching the contextual origins of news events. Instead, they rely on standardized framing, jingoistic rhetoric, and distractions or outright fabrications—all hallmarks of News Abuse that, no matter how inaccurate, are rarely corrected, and almost never come back to discredit the candidates, pollsters, political officials, propagandists or pundits who espouse them.

When corporate media hide or aim to discredit journalistic exposés about the accelerating dangers of online censorship and "content moderation," while celebrating wars that bring the world ever closer to nuclear Armageddon, they demonstrate the worst practices of News Abuse. It is time for corporate media to represent the views and interests of the majority of Americans, instead of repeating the increasingly transparent lies told by those in positions of power and wealth. Until they do so, establishment media bear a significant share of responsibility for the environmental and human destruction wrought by the endless pursuit of elite interests for money and political control.

ROBIN ANDERSEN is a writer, award-winning author, and Professor Emerita of Communication and Media Studies at Fordham University. She edits the Routledge Focus Book Series on Media and Humanitarian Action. Her latest books include *Investigating Death in Paradise: Finding New Meaning in the BBC Mystery Series*, and the forthcoming *Censorship, Digital Media, and the Global Crackdown on Freedom of Expression*. She writes regularly for Fairness and Accuracy in Reporting (FAIR) and is a Project Censored judge.

Notes

1   Billy Witz and Corey Kilgannon, "How George Santos Made Baruch Volleyball Famous," *New York Times*, January 25, 2023.
2   Martin Pengelly, "George Santos: Puppy Theft Charge News Follows Romney's 'Sick Puppy' Barb," *The Guardian*, February 10, 2023.
3   Steven Vago and Jesse O'Neill, "'Clown' Rep.-Elect George Santos Unfit for Congress, NY Protesters Say," *New York Post*, December 29, 2022.
4   Grant Lally, "Small, Local Paper Uncovered and Reported George Santos Scandal before November Election," interview by Geoff Bennett, *PBS NewsHour*, January 9, 2023, audio, 5:40.
5   Jacqueline Sweet, "Feds Probing Santos' Role in Service Dog Charity Scheme," Politico, February 1, 2023; Martin Pengelly, "George Santos Accused of Sexual Harassment by Congressional Aide," *The Guardian*, February 5, 2023.
6   Vago and O'Neill, "'Clown' Rep.-Elect George Santos Unfit."
7   Witz and Kilgannon, "How George Santos Made Baruch Volleyball Famous."
8   Martin Pengelly, "George Santos Is a 'Sociopath,' Fellow New York Republican Congressman Says," *The Guardian*, February 8, 2023; Vago and O'Neill, "'Clown' Rep.-Elect George Santos Unfit."
9   James Bickerton, "George Santos Reelection Bid Sparks Wave of Mocking Memes, Reaction," *Newsweek*, April 18, 2023.
10 Greene boasted that the January 6th mob would have been well-armed and "would have won" if she had been responsible for organizing the insurrection.
11 Marjorie Taylor Greene, interview by Leslie Stahl, *60 Minutes*, April 2, 2023.
12 Eric Hananoki, "Rep. Marjorie Taylor Greene on Facebook in 2018: Parkland School Shooting Was a False Flag Planned Event," Media Matters for America, January 19, 2021, updated January 20, 2021.
13 J. Kim Murphy, "'60 Minutes' Draws Criticism for Marjorie Taylor Greene Interview: 'It's a Failure on CBS,'" *Variety*, April 3, 2023.
14 Jeff Zeleny, "How Marjorie Taylor Greene Landed Seats on Two Key House Committees," CNN, January 18, 2023.
15 Glenn Kessler et al., "In Four Years, President Trump Made 30,573 False or Misleading Claims," *Washington Post*, May 19, 2017, updated January 20, 2021.

16   Terry Spencer, Will Weissert, and Michael R. Sisak, "Trump Arrives in New York Ahead of Expected Arraignment," *PBS NewsHour,* April 3, 2023, updated April 4, 2023.

17   Matt Shuham and Christopher Mathias, "At Trump's Arraignment, a Sad MAGA Circus Mourns the 'Funeral Procession for Our Republic,'" HuffPost, April 4, 2023.

18   U.S. Attorney's Office, Eastern District of New York, "Congressman George Santos Charged with Fraud, Money Laundering, Theft of Public Funds, and False Statements," press release, May 10, 2023.

19   Sheldon Wolin, *Democracy Incorporated: Managed Democracy and the Specter of Inverted Totalitarianism—New Edition* (New Jersey: Princeton University Press, 2017), xxi.

20   Seymour Hersh and Mickey Huff, "Seymour Hersh on Nordstream," interview by Ralph Nader, *Ralph Nader Radio Hour*, February 25, 2023, audio, 1:44:35; quotation by Huff on "corporate capture" at 38:23.

21   Robin Andersen, "Pushing Products and Blaming Consumers: Corporate Journalism, Climate Change, and the Discourses of Delay," in *The Routledge Companion to Advertising and Promotional Culture*, 2nd ed., eds. Emily West and Matthew P. McAllister (New York: Routledge, 2023).

22   David Sirota et al., "Pete Buttigieg Is Pretending He's Powerless to Change Railroad Safety Procedures," *Jacobin*, February 16, 2023.

23   Chris D'Angelo, "Water Testing After Ohio Derailment—Led by Rail Company Itself—Condemned as 'Sloppy,'" HuffPost, February 17, 2023, updated February 18, 2023.

24   "Train Derailment in East Palestine, Ohio," ARL Weekly News (NOAA Air Resources Laboratory), last modified February 24, 2023.

25   David Sirota et al., "Rail Companies Blocked Safety Rules Before Ohio Derailment," The Lever, February 8, 2023.

26   Lee Fang, "Years Before East Palestine Disaster, Congressional Allies of the Rail Industry Intervened to Block Safety Regulations," The Intercept, February 21, 2023.

27   Alison Fisher, "Study: National Television Coverage of East Palestine Train Derailment Ignored Industry Culpability," Media Matters for America, February 14, 2023.

28   Fisher, "Study: National Television Coverage."

29   Thomas Black, "Bungled Messaging Over Ohio Train Crash Causes Chaos," Bloomberg News, February 18, 2023.

30   Andrew Perez, "Buttigieg Pressured Into Promising to Do His Job," The Lever, February 22, 2023.

31   Andrew Perez, "Rail Lobbyists Pay Politico to Tout Train Safety," The Lever, February 28, 2023.

32   Ian Jefferies, "How an American Icon Can Help Solve Three Modern Day Needs," *New York Times*, undated [accessed June 19, 2023]. The *Times* published the Association of American Railroads' paid advertorial with a disclaimer: "The news and editorial staff of The New York Times had no role in this advertisement's creation."

33   Association of American Railroads, "Why Today's Freight Rail Is Safer than Ever," Vox Creative, undated [accessed June 19, 2023]; see also Perez, "Rail Lobbyists Pay Politico to Tout Train Safety."

34   Maximillian Alvarez, "'This Was Preventable': Railroad Workers Explain How Wall St Caused the East Palestine Derailment," The Real News Network, February 23, 2023.

35   Alvarez, "'This Was Preventable.'"

36   Perez, "Rail Lobbyists Pay Politico."

37   Hersh and Huff, interview.

38   David Sirota, et al., "Pete Buttigieg Is Pretending."

39   "Reporter Arrested During Ohio Train Derailment Briefing," Associated Press, February 9, 2023, video, 1:45.

40   Ashleigh Banfield et al., "Experts 'Disturbed' by Force Used on NewsNation Reporter," NewsNation, February 9, 2023.

41   "Journalist Evan Lambert Arrested, Charged While Covering Ohio Train Derailment," Committee to Protect Journalists, February 7, 2023.

42   "United Kingdom: UN Expert Calls for Immediate Release of Assange After 10 Years of Arbitrary Detention," Office of the United Nations High Commissioner for Human Rights Rights (OHCHR), press release, December 8, 2020.

43   James Bovard, "Biden's Atrocious Assange Prosecution," Future of Freedom Foundation, March 1, 2023.

44   Kevin Gosztola, *Guilty of Journalism: The Political Case Against Julian Assange* (Fair Oaks, CA, and New York: The Censored Press and Seven Stories Press, 2023).

45   "Assange to Face Extradition from the United States," Freedom of the Press Foundation, December 10, 2021.

46   Charlie Savage, "Major News Outlets Urge U.S. to Drop Its Charges against Assange," *New York Times*, November 28, 2022, updated November 29, 2022; Kevin John McEvoy, "A Fate Worse Than Censorship: The UK, WikiLeaks, and Julian Assange," in *Censorship, Digital Media and the Global Crackdown on Freedom of Expression*, eds. Robin Andersen, Nolan Higdon, and Steve Macek (New York: Peter Lang, 2024).

47   Eve Ottenberg, "A Free Press in Peril: The Assange Case Drags On," *CounterPunch*, March 24, 2023.

48   "Lawmakers around the World Call On AG Merrick Garland to Drop Charges against Julian Assange," Assange Defense, April 11, 2023.

49   Mickey Huff, "Journalism Is Not a Crime," Dispatches from Project Censored, May 1, 2023; Caitlin Johnstone, "Washington Says 'Journalism is Not a Crime' While Working to Criminalize Journalism," Going Rogue, April 7, 2023, SoundCloud audio, 4:57.

50   John McEvoy and Mark Curtis, "How the UK Media Misinforms Us About 'Counter-Disinformation' Operations," Declassified UK, April 5, 2023.

51   Jessica Corbett, "In Face of US Claims, Moscow Says 'There is No "Russian Invasion" of Ukraine,'" Common Dreams, February 17, 2022.

52   Jake Johnson, "Corporate Media Accused of 'Cheerleading' for US Escalation in Ukraine," Common Dreams, March 18, 2022.

53   Bryce Greene, "In Ukraine, 'No One Hears That There Is a Diplomatic Solution,'" *CounterSpin* interview by Janine Jackson, Fairness & Accuracy in Reporting, February 24, 2022.

54 Bryce Greene, "What You Should *Really* Know About Ukraine," Fairness & Accuracy in Reporting, January 28, 2022.

55 Caitlin Johnstone, "Ukraine Is the Most Aggressively Trolled War of All Time: Notes From the Edge of the Narrative Matrix," Substack, June 30, 2022.

56 Aamer Madhani and Emily Swanson, "Support for Ukraine Softens in U.S. Public, Polls Say," *PBS NewsHour*, February 15, 2023.

57 "Our Photographers in Ukraine on the Images They Can't Forget," *New York Times*, February 24, 2023.

58 Julia Gledhill and William D. Hartung, "Merger Mania in the Military-Industrial Complex," Tomdispatch, February 14, 2023.

59 Tom Engelhardt, "McCarthyism Then and Now," Tomdispatch, February 21, 2023.

60 Patricia Zengerle, "Liberal U.S. Lawmakers Withdraw Ukraine Letter after Blowback," Reuters, October 25, 2022; see also Robin Andersen, "NATO Narratives and Corporate Media Are Leading to 'Doorstep of Doom,'" Fairness & Accuracy in Reporting, December 1, 2022.

61 Robin Andersen, "Beijing's Movie War Propaganda—And Washington's," Fairness & Accuracy in Reporting, December 31, 2021.

62 Jonathan Cook, "Why the Media Don't Want to Know the Truth About the Nord Stream Blasts," MintPress News, April 11, 2023.

63 Bryce Greene, "US Media's Intellectual No-Fly-Zone on US Culpability in Nord Stream Attack," Fairness & Accuracy in Reporting, October 7, 2022.

64 Meg Kelly, Michael Birnbaum, and Mary Ilyushina, "European Leaders Blame Russian 'Sabotage' After Nord Stream Explosions," *Washington Post*, September 27, 2022.

65 Cook, "Why the Media Don't Want to Know the Truth."

66 David McHugh, "What's Russia's Nord Stream 2 Pipeline to Europe?" Associated Press, February 8, 2022.

67 "Live: Ukraine War Testimony to Be Given to US Congress," Independent, January 26, 2023, video, 2:24:50.

68 Greene, "US Media's Intellectual No-Fly-Zone."

69 David Klepper, "Russians Push Baseless Theory Blaming US for Burst Pipeline," Associated Press, September 30, 2022.

70 Caitlin Johnstone, "It's Only a 'Conspiracy Theory' When It Accuses the US Government," CaitlinJohnstone.com, October 4, 2022.

71 Wall Street Silver (@WallStreetSilv), "Professor Sachs on Bloomberg says US did Nordstream and explains evidence, then gets yanked off the air . . . ," Bloomberg TV, October 3, 2022, video, 1:26.

72 Alex Blair, "Columbia Professor Jeffery Sachs Yanked off Air after Accusing US of Sabotaging Nord Stream Pipeline," *New York Post*, October 4, 2022.

73 Greene, "US Media's Intellectual No-Fly-Zone."

74 Seymour Hersh, "How America Took Out the Nord Steam Pipeline," Substack, February 8, 2023.

75 "White House Says Blog Post on Nord Stream Explosion 'Utterly False'," Reuters, February 8, 2023.

76 Ross Douthat, "U.F.O.s and Other Unsolved Mysteries of Our Time," *New York Times*, February 15, 2023.

77   John Yoo and Robert Delahunty, "Constitutional Hypocrisy and the
      Nord Stream 2 Explosion," *Newsweek*, February 14, 2023.

78   Patrick Lawrence, "Totalized Censorship," Consortium News, February
      20, 2023; see also Andy Lee Roth and Mickey Huff, "Fake News: Who
      Checks the Fact Checkers?" in *Project Censored's State of the Free Press
      2021*, eds. Mickey Huff and Andy Lee Roth (New York: Seven Stories
      Press, 2020), 8-10.

79   Alan MacLeod, "Meet the Ex-CIA Agents Deciding Facebook's Con-
      tent Policy," MintPress News, July 12, 2022; "National Security Search
      Engine: Google's Ranks Are Filled With CIA Agents," MintPress News,
      July 25, 2022; and "The Federal Bureau of Tweets: Twitter Is Hiring an
      Alarming Number of FBI Agents," MintPress News, June 21, 2022. See
      "Censored" Story #2 in Chapter 1 of this volume for Project Censored's
      coverage of MacLeod's reporting.

80   Moira Feldman and Rob Williams, "Russiagate: Two-Headed Monster
      of Propaganda and Censorship," in *Censored 2019: Fighting the Fake
      News Invasion*, eds. Mickey Huff and Andy Lee Roth (New York: Seven
      Stories Press, 2018), 54-56; accessible online in Project Censored's archive
      of its annual Top 25 story lists.

81   Andy Lee Roth, avram anderson, and Mickey Huff, "Beyond Prior
      Restraint: Censorship by Proxy and the New Digital Gatekeeping,"
      Dispatches from Project Censored, February 9, 2023.

82   "Exposure to Russian Twitter Campaigns in 2016 Presidential Race
      Highly Concentrated, Largely Limited to Strongly Partisan Republi-
      cans," New York University, news release, January 9, 2023.

83   Jeff Gerth, "The Press Versus the President, Part One," *Columbia Jour-
      nalism Review*, January 30, 2023.

84   Jeremy Scahill, "The Disturbing Groupthink Over the War in Ukraine,"
      The Intercept, March 3, 2023.

85   Branko Marcetic, "Today's Hawkish Discourse Makes the Cuban Missile
      Crisis's Nuclear Brinkmanship Seem Sane," *Jacobin*, October 30, 2022.

CHAPTER 5

Media Democracy in Action

Contributions by MARIA ARMOUDIAN and OLIVIA
GUYODO (University of Auckland), CHRISTINE EMERAN
(National Coalition Against Censorship), JEN SENKO (*The
Brainwashing of My Dad*), and REBECCA VINCENT
(Reporters Without Borders)

Introduction by MISCHA GERACOULIS

In early 2023, the thirty-ninth president of the United
States, Jimmy Carter, aged ninety-eight, made public his
decision to retreat into hospice care. By springtime, political activist Daniel Ellsberg, aged ninety-two, publicized a
similar decision before his passing on June 16, 2023. By all
accounts, Ellsberg remained engaged and true to his convictions to the very end.[1] Renowned for demonstrations
of unyielding moral courage undertaken at great personal
risk, both Carter and Ellsberg are distinguished by lifelong commitments to peacebuilding, truth-telling, and
democracy that leave an indelible imprint, not only on US
democracy but on democracies worldwide.[2]

Central to the legacy they bestow upon succeeding
generations is the import and function of free and ethical journalism that upholds citizens' rights to accurate
information and full civic engagement. These two elder
statesmen are passing on a torch that, in the grand pop-
ulace of life, a scattered few are willing to take up. In

recognition of their service and the esteem in which they've held the Fourth Estate, this chapter spotlights those who dare to assume the next incarnation of mantles long carried by Jimmy Carter and Dan Ellsberg.

The work of the following torchbearers offers points of light in a world currently under the shadow of extremism, polarization, and unabashed misinformation, disinformation, and malinformation. In service to rights-based democracies, these individuals and organizations work to uphold the guardrails of free and independent media currently under threat by repressive regimes, right-wing movements, corporate media mergers, and divisive politics, nationally and globally.

According to Reporters Without Borders' (RSF) 2023 *World Press Freedom Index*, the quality of journalism, the safety of journalists, press freedoms, and even the security of nations, as academics Maria Armoudian and Olivia Guyodo highlight in this chapter, are adversely impacted by the "fake content industry." Of the 180 countries evaluated by RSF's *Index*, 118 countries reported that political actors were often or systematically involved in massive disinformation or propaganda campaigns, obscuring the difference between true and false, real and fake, and facts and artifices, altogether jeopardizing citizens' right to information.[3]

In the case of the Azerbaijani regime's attack on the autonomous region of Artsakh, as Armoudian and Guyodo illuminate, the basic human right to ethnic identity and existence is also jeopardized. The RSF *Index* ranks Azerbaijan at 151 (of 180) in terms of press freedom and describes President Ilham Aliyev as actively seeking to erase any vestige of ethnic and media pluralism. No one understands the gravity of RSF's annual indexing more profoundly than the organization's director of campaigns, Rebecca Vincent, whose contribution to this chapter examines national security worldwide in the context of journalist safety, press freedom, and factual reporting.

Around the world, Vincent explains, journalists, media professionals, activists, and educators are targeted under the guise of national security as governments invoke or invent legislation to suppress the media and public information intrinsic to any democracy. One such case that Vincent discusses is the United States Espionage Act, which factors into the *Index*'s ranking for US press freedom. Broadly speaking, the US media landscape is free from governmental intrusion. However, the largest media outlets are consolidated and owned by a handful of wealthy individuals, and local news outlets continue a downward spiral, contributing to the 2023 *Index* calculations that ranked the United States in forty-fifth position.

Recognizing that local news is fundamental to the public sphere, governmental checks-and-balances, civic engagement, and public health and safety, news deserts are an increasing issue of concern in the United States. Documentary filmmaker Jen Senko monitors the destructive impacts of news deserts and the right-wing-dominant media environment on individual and societal health. Part of Senko's work in media democracy has been to reveal the strategically organized steps undertaken by conservative billionaires, media moguls, and government officials intent on upending media pluralism in the United States. Her essay makes clear that the implementation of the "Fox News model" of propaganda and outright deception has taken hold not by chance but by design. The sheer volume and intensity of fake news pumped out of Fox networks, amplified by repetition across social media and other online echo chambers, is a proven recipe for brainwashing, capable of inducing citizens to vote against their own best interests.

This right-wing agenda is by no means limited to the realm of news. Director of the Youth Free Expression Program at the National Coalition Against Censorship, Christine Emeran, highlights state and national efforts that target education. Perpetuating dissension, parochialism, and "othering," ultra-conservative lawmakers and their constituents have seized on public educational curricula and library materials. Emeran details myriad ways that millions of students are being affected by newly enacted laws that curtail learning, restrict access to information, and challenge or ban books by the hundreds, thus undermining fundamental rights to quality education and access to accurate information.

After a book-burning event in 1933 Berlin that included the destruction of titles by American author Helen Keller, Keller wrote in the *New York Times* that no matter how many books get burned, ideas would not be killed.[4] Although book bans may not be the same as book burnings, the premise is the same, establishing dictates as to what and who is acceptable and what histories and narratives are advanced. But, as Keller contended, there will always be other ways to permeate minds and quicken ideas. This year's Media Democracy in Action contributors are exemplary in that regard, each utilizing the channels of media, education, government, and law to quicken democratic ideas and ideals.

Remarking in 2021 on his appreciation for the US First

Amendment, Ellsberg asserted that without the protection for freedom of the press and freedom of thought, a democracy can't survive.[5] Moreover, freedom is not free, and with rights come responsibilities. Correspondingly, in a 2022 *New York Times* op-ed, Carter called for a renewal of respect for democratic norms, safe and fair participation in elections, and efforts to counter disinformation.[6] The torch Carter and Ellsberg pass along to the next generation is not for the faint of heart, but the issues they dedicated their lives to addressing can be resolved. The work of the determined women featured here offers possibilities for recourse, pathways forward, and cause for optimism. Readers will find inspiration and reasons to partake in protecting and promoting fair and equitable media and educational systems, journalistic and communication standards, and all the mechanisms for accessing information and verifying facts.

This chapter is dedicated to the legacies of Jimmy Carter and Daniel Ellsberg and to anyone anywhere who has the audacity to employ media for democratic ends.

MISCHA GERACOULIS is a journalist and editor who serves as contributing editor at *The Markaz Review* and on the editorial board of the Censored Press. Her research concentrates on the intersections among critical media and information literacy, human rights education, and democracy and ethics. Her priority issues of focus include truth in reporting, press and academic freedoms, the protracted disinformation campaign against the Armenian Genocide, and diasporic identities and culture.

HOW CENSORSHIP IS WIELDED FOR THE SILENCING AND ATTEMPTED ERASURE OF A PEOPLE

MARIA ARMOUDIAN AND OLIVIA GUYODO

Traditional censorship—when governments overtly suppress or ban the press or aspects of realities that they consider objectionable—is one way of preventing knowledge or multiple perspectives from reaching audiences. This occurs in authoritarian regimes and so-called democracies, such as Turkey and Azerbaijan. But Western countries' media suppress and skew information and perspectives too—namely through their framing, economic structures, and norms that often prioritize profits and uphold the status quo.

Driven to amass audiences, which helps secure funding, many media publish and frame stories for mass appeal. This usually means matters of novelty; exciting, dramatic, or conflictual stories; and the antics of famous people. Although these practices are not direct censorship, they leave little room for reporting that helps audiences understand substantial issues. Whether inadvertent or intentional, the result is the same: As weightier information is silenced or drowned out, people may remain unapprised of consequential, even life-and-death, issues.

Such omissions have added to the suffering of the ethnic Armenians in the South Caucuses region that borders Eastern Europe and Western Asia. The region called "Artsakh" in the Armenian language and "Nagorno Karabakh" internationally, is a sliver—approximately 1,700 square miles—of what's left of the indigenous Armenian homeland. For historical context, Armenians had already lost most of their ancestral land and cultural heritage sites to Ottoman Turkey, which committed pogroms, slaughters, and other egregious human rights violations on Armenians before, during, and after the 1915 Armenian Genocide.

Under Soviet rule in 1923, as part of his divide-and-conquer policies, Josef Stalin declared the Armenian-populated Artsakh (Nagorno Karabakh) an autonomous region, separate from the rest of Armenia, and placed it within the territorial boundaries of Azerbaijan. For years, Armenians in Artsakh and neighboring Armenia called for reunification. When the 1991 fall of the Soviet Union legally ended the territorial designations, Azerbaijan refused to accept Artsakh's autonomy, prompting Artsakh's independence movement and eventual war of independence. Tens of thousands of Armenians and Azerbaijanis lost their lives in that war; however, indigenous Armenians held fast and established a de facto democracy.

After Azerbaijan's post-Soviet independence, the Aliyev political family exercised authoritarian control in the nation. Freedom House, an international organization that measures political freedoms, scored Azerbaijan with nine points out of one hundred for political rights and civil liberties.[7] Under Ilham Aliyev, president since 2003, Azerbaijan's media has disseminated a vehemently anti-Armenian official line, characterizing Armenians as fascists, animals, terrorists, and illegal occupiers—a tried and true means of building support for violent war.[8]

In 2020, with Turkey's backing, Azerbaijan attacked the Armenians in Artsakh, using conventional weaponry alongside banned cluster munitions, drone technology, and mercenaries. By the end of the forty-four-day war, the victor, Azerbaijan, launched an ethnic cleansing campaign in Artsakh, driving ethnic Armenians from their homes and looting, appropriating, and destroying Armenian cultural heritage sites.[9] All the while, Azerbaijani media promoted the country as multicultural, accused Armenians of aggression, and falsified the region's history.[10]

Yet, much of the world has hardly noticed. Both Azerbaijan and Turkey control and censor information within and beyond their borders, disseminating false narratives about Armenians. Journalists and peace advocates in Azerbaijan and Turkey who dare to work on reconciliation issues with Armenia risk reprisals. For example, in 2014, Azerbaijani human rights activist and director of the Institute for Peace and Democracy, Leyla Yunus, and her husband, Arif Yunus, visited Armenia for dialogue and peacebuilding. Upon their return to Azerbaijan, they were arrested and charged with espionage and collaboration with Armenia over the Artsakh conflict.[11]

The Republic of Turkey similarly uses state control to suppress truths and revise its past. Although modern Turkey was built through genocide of the region's indigenous Armenians, Assyrians, and Greeks, Turkish law criminalizes publication of this history. Article 301 of the Turkish penal code prohibits "insulting Turkishness," which includes acknowledging the Armenian Genocide. And Law 7262, "On the Prevention of the Financing of Weapons of Mass Destruction," enables the state to target civil society under the guise of preventing terrorist activities.

Since 1992, more than 420 journalists have been attacked in Turkey, twenty-six of whom have been killed, and 377 imprisoned, at the time of this publication, mostly for "anti-state" reporting, according to the Committee to Protect Journalists.[12] The initial 2017 arrest and 2022 life sentence of Turkish philanthropist and rights activist, Osman Kavala, exemplifies the country's tactics. Committed to improving relations with Armenians and other ethnic minorities in Turkey, Kavala, to his detriment, had acknowledged the Armenian Genocide.

Outside of their borders, Azerbaijan and Turkey spend millions to cover up their past and present war crimes through lobbying in Western nations, advertising in Western media, public relations, and diplomacy. In 2020, the year the two countries coordinated to attack Artsakh, Turkey and Azerbaijan together spent more than $8 million in lobbying the United States alone.[13] After the US Congress introduced resolutions condemning the attacks, Azerbaijan hired the public relations firm Portland PR, paying $30,000 per month to manage the narrative.[14]

Meanwhile, most Western media failed to cover Azerbaijan's war on Artsakh. Scant reporting, such as that by the *New York Times*, basically amounted to what some media scholars call "stenography." Reports excluded historical context, analysis, and critical thinking, and some adopted one-sided framing of Azerbaijan and Turkey, quoting condemnations of Armenia by Turkey's president, Recep Erdogan, without context or rebuttal. While this is not official censorship, reporting that is stripped of vital information confirms biases and spreads propaganda, contributes to Azerbaijan's and Turkey's crusades against the Armenian people, and betrays the journalistic standards and ethics expected in a democracy.

MARIA ARMOUDIAN is Senior Lecturer of politics and international relations and co-director of Ngā Ara Whetū Centre for Climate, Biodiversity and Society at the University of Auckland. She is the founder of the *Scholars' Circle* radio program and author of three books, *Lawyers Beyond Borders: Advancing International Human Rights through Local Laws and Courts; Reporting from the Danger Zone: Frontline Journalists, Their Jobs and Increasingly Perilous Future;* and *Kill the Messenger: The Media's Role in the Fate of the World.*

OLIVIA GUYODO is a graduate student at the University of Auckland, currently completing her M.A. in politics and international relations. Her studies focus on collective memory and the state, the media, and the erasure of cultural heritage with a special interest in the Caucasus region.

CENSORING BOOKS IN SCHOOLS HITS A CRISIS POINT

CHRISTINE EMERAN

The last few years have seen a sharp rise in organized, politically-driven efforts to ban books in US schools. Variously led by parents, community members, political action groups, and lawmakers, such efforts target books with LGBTQ, sex, gender, or race-related content. In some instances, books have been singled out for individual passages or images, disregarding the book's literary and educational value as a whole. Data from the American Library Association recorded 729 challenges to 1,597 titles in 2021, spiking to more than 1,200 challenges to 2,500 titles in 2022.[15]

Since 2021, conservative lawmakers in seventeen states

have enacted laws or rules to counter the "inculcation of" or "indoctrination in" divisive ideas. Schools are citing these laws and policies as reasons to exclude LGBTQ, race, racism, sex, and gender identity subject matter from the curricula and even school libraries. As a result, according to the National Coalition Against Censorship's Youth Censorship Database, public schools in forty-five US states have been impacted, affecting millions of students.

Emily Knox, information sciences professor at the University of Illinois, Urbana-Champaign, has asserted that a book is "a symbolic object of authority." Books, Knox writes, "contain limitless content and ideas," making them "simultaneously a stabilizing and destabilizing force in society."[16] This force could explain efforts in states governed by Republicans to remove books with ideas interpreted as threats to their particular vision of societal order.[17] Often, these legislators invoke "parents' rights" as a mobilizing tool to justify the censorship of contested viewpoints in education.

Conservative groups and legislators nationwide are responsible for recent state bills that censor or suppress discussions on race, slavery, oppression, gender, and LGBTQ subject matter, target critical race theory (CRT), and ban books with so-called "sexually explicit" content. PEN America reports that fifty-four divisive concepts, or anti-CRT bills, have been proposed in forty-four states, seventeen of which have been adopted in eight states, according to *Time*.[18]

Florida's Parental Rights in Education Act (House Bill 1557), known to critics as the "Don't Say Gay" bill, restricts classroom discussion about gender or sexuality from kindergarten to third grade. It also requires educators to report to parents any gender or sexuality information disclosed by students and requires public schools to pay legal costs of parental lawsuits if schools violate the law.[19] In Missouri, it is now a crime to distribute "sexually explicit" images to minors, which has resulted in districts pulling some three hundred books with visual content, including certain graphic novels, from their shelves.[20] Such laws are vague, unclear in their enforcement, and create an atmosphere of fear in schools and public libraries where employees may face retaliation from lawmakers or community members.

In recent years, strategies typically employed by parents who challenge books through school boards have expanded to involve community members without children in the school district. These challenges are not only to individual titles, but also include long lists of "objectionable" titles sourced from lists published by conservative political action groups, such as Moms for Liberty. The group's national campaign advocates for the mass removal of books, working under the banner of "protecting minors from age-inappropriate material."[21] Families, community members, and advocacy groups have criticized Moms for Liberty and other organizations for their ties to networks within the Republican party and for using the party's tactics to impose ideological constraints on public schools and libraries.

In reaction to the political onslaught, some school administrators have removed dozens of books without subjecting them to a formal review process, presumably to avoid controversy or penalty for violating new state laws.[22] There has been pushback to these bans by advocacy groups such as the National Coalition Against Censorship, through local community action, and most notably, by student-led protests.

In 2022, Pennsylvania students Edha Gupta, Christina Ellis, and others from Central York High School founded an anti-racism club to challenge a ban on educational materials that offer culturally diverse perspectives. After months of protests, the students convinced the district to permit the use of the materials.[23] In Katy Independent School District in Texas, student Cameron Samuels responded to the district's ban on LGBTQ resources by speaking out at a school board meeting, mobilizing other students to do the same, and organizing a banned book drive. Their efforts succeeded in the district's decision to unblock some of the internet filters, enabling students to access LGBTQ resources from school computers.[24] In early 2023, high school students in Canby, Oregon, protested the removal of approximately thirty books from school libraries.[25] And dozens of students from Big Walnut High School in Sunbury, Ohio, protested the banning of twenty "explicit" books by staging a peaceful school walkout.[26]

Censorship of books and ideas is a repressive tactic when used by the state and political actors to assert more control over young people, impose a conservative political ideology on public education, and disingenuously prioritize parental rights above educators' professional expertise. Divisive concepts and laws overlook the lived experiences of marginalized students and function to restrict students' access to information and material that may be culturally affirming or even lifesaving. Ultimately, the burden of this political and ideological strife is borne by students whose need to read broadly and learn about a changing world is denied. There is no end in sight to the current struggle, and the people who are fighting censorship need all the help they can get. To learn more, visit Unite Against Book Bans www.uniteagainstbookbans.org.

CHRISTINE EMERAN is director of the Youth Free Expression Program at the National Coalition Against Censorship. She writes on contemporary issues about young people, social media, and social movements in the United States and Europe. Emeran is a Fulbright Fellow and author of *New Generation Political Activism in Ukraine: 2000–2014*, and a book chapter on generational change and the personalization of protest, included in a global social movement book series, *When Students Protest: Secondary and High Schools*. She has taught at Manhattan College and St. John's University in New York; Sciences Po in Paris, France; and received a PhD in sociology from the New School for Social Research.

A MOVIE, A BOOK, AND A LIFE OF ACTIVISM, THANKS TO MY DAD'S BRAINWASHING BY RIGHT-WING MEDIA

JEN SENKO

My father's disturbing changes started with Rush Limbaugh and only got worse when he found Fox "News." (I put "News" in quotes based on research for my film, *The Brainwashing of My Dad*, but more on that later.) After a subsequent barrage of emails parroting Limbaugh and Fox, my dad went completely off the rails. I likened the change he underwent to the 1950s movie, *Invasion of the Body Snatchers*, as my previously easygoing, politically liberal father had suddenly turned explosive anytime anyone challenged his new, yet seemingly deeply held, ultra-conservative views. It wasn't just his personality or his politics that radically changed—most distressing was the change in his relationship to us, his family.

After witnessing other people metamorphose as my dad had, it became chillingly clear to me this wasn't just happenstance but that an orchestrated, targeted campaign was underway. The right-wing media, to which my dad and others I knew had subscribed, had them convinced that Democrats and Democratic policies are evil, incompetent, and corrupt. Because of my experience in documentary filmmaking, I determined that my next film *had* to be *The Brainwashing of My Dad*. I needed to find out the who and why behind this media-centered attempt to divide our country that demonized anything "Democrat," and most importantly, how they managed to dominate the media.

After the 2016 release of *The Brainwashing of My Dad*, I worried that not enough people comprehended the extent of the media crisis. So, I wrote an updated book version of the film, using the same name, thinking a book might garner wider attention. In my book and film, and ensuing interviews and written pieces, I show how specific historical events paved the way for a right-wing political takeover. The Right understood that by gaining control of the media, they could change—or worse, brainwash—a lot of minds.

An Orchestrated and Targeted Campaign

Consider the John Birch Society, founded in 1958 by Robert W. Welch Jr. (1899–1985), funded in part by Fred

Koch, and supported by then-presidential nominee, Barry Goldwater. Seen by the general public as an extreme fringe group, "Birchers" railed against communism and pushed a far-right libertarian agenda. Due in part to Goldwater's support for the Birchers, Lyndon Johnson won the 1964 presidential election by a landslide. Reacting to Goldwater's defeat and pronouncements that the Right was dead, Reed Irvine, conservative activist and economist, founded the media watchdog organization Accuracy In Media (AIM) in 1969. Intentionally labeling the establishment media as "liberal," AIM laid the groundwork for the rise of "conservative media."

While Richard Nixon was campaigning for the US presidency in the 1960s, he met Roger Ailes, a brilliant, up-and-coming television producer, who groomed Nixon to be more media savvy, thereby winning the election. After Nixon appointed Ailes as his television adviser, Ailes presented a secret memo to the Nixon White House titled "A Plan for Putting the GOP on TV News." It outlined how to create "GOP TV" and cast pro-Republican ideas in the most favorable light.

In 1971, the US Chamber of Commerce hired corporate lawyer Lewis Powell to strategize the advancement of the free-market economy doctrine and end the social and civil rights movements of the time. The top-secret Powell memo made clear that a coordinated plan was underway to drive the country to the political Right through corporate- and billionaire-backed political action and acquisition and domination of the media.[27]

Then in 1981, in a one-two punch, President Ronald Reagan, granted US citizenship to Australian billionaire and media mogul Rupert Murdoch and vetoed codification of the 1949 Fairness Doctrine that had required public broadcasters to provide multiple and opposing views on controversial issues of public importance. The Fairness Doctrine's end cleared the way for national syndication of the "Rush Limbaugh Show." Gaining access to AM and FM airwaves nationwide, including the Armed Forces Network radio, the right-wing shock jock was able to freely peddle incendiary speech, fake news, and conspiracy theories on a daily basis.

The 1996 Telecommunications Act, signed into law by President Bill Clinton, obliterated Roosevelt's 1934 Communications Act, which until then had prevented media ownership consolidation. Seven months later, Rupert Murdoch hired none other than Roger Ailes to manufacture one of the most influential propaganda machines ever—Fox "News." A master propagandist, having studied the cinematography tactics of Nazi propagandist Leni Riefenstahl, Ailes launched a sophisticated propaganda scheme to fuel the conservative agenda, and persuade Fox viewers to vote Republican, even if that meant voting against their best interests.

Fabricating "in-groups" and "out-groups" and spotlighting Democrats, Black and Brown people, poor people, and immigrants as the ultimate, fearsome outgroups worked to whip up irrational fears. Coupled with the staging of Fox anchors feigning on-air outrage, Ailes (like Nazi politician and propaganda minister Joseph Goebbels) knew that audiences would be triggered into emotional fight or flight. With rational thinking out the window, audiences were primed to receive Fox's messaging. Sinclair Broadcast Group, which owned or operated 192 television stations in eighty-nine US markets, according to a 2018 report in the *New Yorker*, is another key player in this contrived "rage-otainment" complex.[28] Employing similar demonizing tactics, their media often wields hate, lies, and division.

The Reaction of Establishment Media and Many Democrats

Corporate media too often reacts like the apologetic victim in an abusive relationship. Sometimes unwittingly playing the part by "both-sides-ing" or pandering to the Right, they practically bend over backward so as not to appear "liberal."

My movie's main purpose was to alert the public that this swing to the Right was not organic but by design. Following the film, I've continued this mission through my book and website, engaging on social media, and by offering free film screenings. Though I'd held screenings every few months since the film's 2016 release, during the COVID-19 lockdown, I provided free screenings via Zoom for advocacy groups that concentrate on important issues outside of media. I did this because I believe what media scholar Robert McChesney said to be true: "Whatever your first issue of concern, media had better be your second, because without change in the media, progress in your primary area is far less likely."[29] To me, this means that if we don't confront right-wing media head-on, we risk losing our democracy.

Some of those advocacy groups have since shifted their focus to media issues, which gives me hope. Having learned from Republicans that there is strength in numbers, I introduced these groups to one another and to other media activists. Another hopeful sign is the $787 million settlement paid to Dominion Voting Systems by Fox "News" for deliberately lying about Dominion's voting machines in the 2020 US presidential election, followed by Fox's firing of Tucker Carlson. And VoteVets, the political action committee for progressive veterans and civilians, has a powerful video ad, calling for Fox's removal from US military bases.[30]

The demise of independent, local news outlets in communities around the country means that conservative, syndicated media is all that's available in some areas. Because the Sinclair network has swept in to fill this void, we must do what we can to support independent media, push corporate media to be more objective, weaken right-wing media's stronghold, and get the Telecommunications Act restored. Let Fox be just the start.

JEN SENKO is an award-winning documentary filmmaker and media activist. Her documentaries are *Road Map Warrior Women* (2000), *The Vanishing City* (2010), and *The Brainwashing of My Dad* (narrated by Matthew Modine, 2016), which tracked the divisive and dangerous rise of right-wing media and how it wreaked havoc on American families and our democracy. *The Brainwashing of My Dad* won the 2021 Webby People's Voice Award for Public Service & Activism and was adapted into a critically-acclaimed book.

CAMPAIGNING TO PROTECT JOURNALISM IN THE ERA OF NATIONAL SECURITY

REBECCA VINCENT

At Reporters Without Borders (RSF), we work globally for the freedom, pluralism, and independence of journalism. To do so, we engage in a wide range of daily activities—from behind-the-scenes advocacy interventions to public mobilization campaigns and everything in between. We provide concrete assistance to journalists, including protective equipment, training, and legal and financial support, and help them fight back when they are targeted. We work hard to hold state and non-state actors to account, end impunity for crimes against journalists, and ensure better proactive protections for journalists going forward. We name and shame when it is merited, but we also talk directly to governments around the world—even the worst offenders, such as Saudi Arabia.

As Director of Campaigns, my role is to strategize and implement our global priority campaigns in coordination with our whole international team. To effectively address our most crucial priorities, we need all hands on deck. Colleagues in departments across our Paris headquarters, as well as RSF's thirteen country bureaus and sections, and a network of correspondents in more than 130 countries all mobilize toward a common objective when needed most.

One of RSF's priority global campaigns is focused on "national security versus journalism." Through this campaign we work to highlight cases from around the world in which journalists have been targeted for national security reasons, putting an international spotlight on this growing problem, and developing recommendations for both governments and journalists. We examine problematic legislation, such as the United States Espionage Act and the National Security Bill in the United Kingdom, and engage in advocacy to secure journalistic protections. We take up cases from around the world, supporting journalists who find themselves targeted in the name of national security, such as Jimmy Lai in Hong Kong, publisher of *Apple Daily* newspaper, and Can Dundar, exiled Turkish editor. And, of course, RSF continues to campaign for the release of WikiLeaks publisher Julian Assange.

RSF has worked to defend Assange from the very start of the US government's case against him, following WikiLeaks's publication of hundreds of thousands of leaked classified diplomatic and military documents in 2010. We launched a more intense campaign around the start of the extradition proceedings against him in London courts in February 2020.

We campaign in support of Assange because he has been targeted for his contributions to journalism. WikiLeaks's publication of the leaked classified documents informed extensive public interest reporting around the world, exposing war crimes and human rights violations that have never been prosecuted. If the United States government is successful in extraditing Assange to the US and prosecuting him there, he would be the first publisher tried under the Espionage Act, which lacks a public interest defense. This would set an alarming precedent that could be applied to any publisher, journalist, or source anywhere in the world.

For the past three years, RSF has worked tirelessly to gain access to and monitor extradition proceedings in various London courts, which have been the hardest to access of any case we have monitored in any country. We battled and exposed a constantly evolving series of court-imposed obstacles that constituted barriers to open justice and the right to a fair trial. We were the only nongovernmental organization that consistently fought for this access and monitored all stages of the extradition proceedings.

In April 2023, RSF hit yet another ludicrous barrier to our work on this case, when the Belmarsh Prison governor revoked the access we had been granted to visit Assange in prison, despite being scheduled weeks in advance and following all prison rules and procedures. This seemingly arbitrary decision violates Assange's right to receive visitors in prison and our ability to do our job as an NGO working on his case. Assange has been largely isolated during his four years of imprisonment, including long stretches with no visitation at all due to the COVID-19 pandemic. Especially considering the severe mental and physical health issues he faces, RSF is concerned about his well-being.

At the time of publication, we await the UK High Court's decision on whether it will consider Assange's appeal against the extradition order signed by the UK Home Secretary in July 2022. If an appeal is allowed, there are several possible outcomes; if it is not accepted, Assange will come dangerously closer to extradition.

In the meantime, RSF is poised to monitor any further UK court proceedings pending the High Court's decision and is fighting the revocation of our visitation access to Assange in Belmarsh Prison. We are engaging in advocacy with the US, UK, and Australian governments, calling on the Biden administration to drop the charges and close the case and urging Australian Prime Minister Albanese to do everything in his power to secure a diplomatic solution for Assange's release without further delay.

We continue our campaign to inform and mobilize the public on this crucial case, which will prove to be a historically definitive test of national security versus journalism that will have lasting global implications no matter the outcome. When publishers or journalists are targeted in this way, it is ultimately the public and democracy that lose out, as everyone has the right to information. To effectively fight back for the protection of all our rights, we need the public's support.

REBECCA VINCENT is Director of Campaigns for Reporters Without Borders (RSF), which acts globally to defend the freedom, pluralism, and independence of journalism. She is an American-British human rights campaigner and former diplomat who has worked with a wide range of nongovernmental organizations and coordinated many high-profile international human rights campaigns.

Notes

1   Robert Ellsberg and Chris Zimmerman, "A Father's Legacy to His Son—And His Country," *Plough*, June 16, 2023.
2   Ellsberg wrote an article for the Media Democracy in Action chapter of the 2014 yearbook. See Daniel Ellsberg, "On Civil Courage and Its Punishments," in *Censored 2014: Fearless Speech in Fateful Times*, eds. Mickey Huff and Andy Lee Roth (New York: Seven Stories, 2013), 208-13, accessible online at the Project Censored website.
3   "2023 World Press Freedom Index—Journalism Threatened by Fake Content Industry," Reporters Without Borders, May 3, 2023.
4   See Josh Jones, "Helen Keller Writes a Letter to Nazi Students Before They Burn Her Book: 'History Has Taught You Nothing if You Think You Can Kill Ideas'(1933)," Open Culture, May 16, 2017.
5   "The Pentagon Papers at 50: Press Freedom and Whistleblowers Still at Risk," *Democracy Now!*, June 17, 2021.
6   Jimmy Carter, "I Fear for Our Democracy," *New York Times*, January 5, 2022.

7   "Freedom in the World 2023, Azerbaijan," Freedom House, 2023.

8   "President Ilham Aliyev Addressed the Nation," Azertac (Azerbaijan State News Agency), October 17, 2020.

9   "General Report," Human Rights Ombudsman of the Republic of Artsakh, October 26, 2020; "Azerbaijan: Unlawful Strikes in Nagorno-Karabakh," Human Rights Watch, December 11, 2020.

10   Vafa Ismayilova, "UN Alerted About Armenian Vandalism Against Azerbaijani Heritage," AzerNews, May 19, 2021.

11   "Case History: Leyla Yunis," Frontline Defenders, December 8, 2014 [updated April 19, 2016].

12   "Journalists Attacked in Turkey Between 1992-2023," Committee to Protect Journalists, undated [accessed May 16, 2023].

13   "Turkey 2020," OpenSecrets, undated [accessed May 16, 2023].

14   Theodoric Meyer and Daniel Lippman, "Azerbaijan Gets Some Public Relations Help," Politico, October 30, 2020.

15   Raymond Garcia, "American Library Association Reports Record Number of Demands to Censor Library Books and Materials in 2022," ALA News (American Library Association), March 22, 2023.

16   Emily J. M. Knox, *Book Banning in 21st-Century America* (Lanham, MD: Rowman & Littlefield, 2015), 31.

17   Ronald Brownstein, "Book Bans Move to Center Stage in the Red-State Education Wars," CNN, April 5, 2022.

18   Jonathan Friedman and James Tager, "Educational Gag Orders: Legislative Restrictions on the Freedom to Read, Learn, and Teach," PEN America, February 25, 2022; Olivia B. Waxman, "Anti-'Critical Race Theory' Laws Are Working. Teachers Are Thinking Twice about How They Talk about Race," *Time*, June 30, 2022.

19   Judd Legum, "Florida Teachers Told to Remove Books from Classroom Libraries or Risk Felony Prosecution," Popular Information, January 23, 2023.

20   Audrey Ghosh, "New Missouri Law Bans Schools from Providing 'Explicit Sexual Content,'" Pathfinder, August 30, 2022; Eesha Pendharkar, "Nearly 300 Books Removed from Schools under Missouri's 'Sexually Explicit Materials' Law," *Education Week*, November 20, 2022; Jodi Fortino and Kate Grumke, "ACLU Sues Missouri over Book Ban Law That Pushed School Libraries to Remove Hundreds of Titles," KCUR (NPR affiliate, Kansas City, MO), February 23, 2023.

21   Jonathan Friedman and Nadine Farid Johnson, "Banned in the USA: The Growing Movement to Censor Books in Schools," PEN America, September 19, 2022.

22   Joan Walsh, "Florida Teachers Hide Their Books to Avoid Felonies," *The Nation*, February 1, 2023.

23   Isabella Grullón Paz and Maria Cramer, "How Students Fought a Book Ban and Won, for Now," *New York Times*, October 2, 2021.

24   Kennedy Ryan, "Fighting Censorship in Katy: Cameron Samuels '26," BrandeisNOW, January 23, 2023.

25   Evan Watson, "Students Protest after Canby School District Removes 35 Books from School Libraries," KGW8 (NBC affiliate, Portland, OR) March 22, 2023.

26   Lu Ann Stoia, "Big Walnut Students Stage Protest over Book Ban
      Effort," WSYX (ABC affiliate, Columbus, OH), January 13, 2023.
27   *Confidential Memorandum: Attack on American Free Enterprise System*,
      Education Committee, US Chamber of Commerce, August 23, 1971.
28   Sheelah Kolhatkar, "The Growth of Sinclair's Conservative Media
      Empire," *New Yorker*, October 15, 2018.
29   Robert McChesney, "Waging the Media Battle," *American Prospect*, June
      17, 2004. McChesney credits the idea to former Federal Communications
      Commission member Nicholas Johnson.
30   VoteVets, "Ban Carlson, Ingraham, and Hannity from All Military Facili-
      ties," YouTube, March 6, 2023, video, 2:19.

CHAPTER 6

Call It What You Want
Journalism, Truth, and Making Media That Empowers Working People[1]

MAXIMILLIAN ALVAREZ

I've always been uncomfortable calling myself a journalist. Part of that has to do with the fact that I perpetually feel like, through equal parts luck and accident, I sort of snuck into this work through the side door. I never went to "J-school," never interned at a major news outlet, and the people who did know this about me. But I think a bigger part of that discomfort comes from the way I approach the work that I do.

At the Real News Network (TRNN) we cover a wide range of topics. We are, I'm proud to say, a true multimedia network, producing original podcasts, like *The Marc Steiner Show*, *Working People*, and *Art for the End Times*, and original YouTube shows, like *Rattling the Bars* (founded and cohosted by legendary Black Panther Eddie Conway, who was wrongfully imprisoned for forty-four years and just recently passed away earlier this year), *The Police Accountability Report* (hosted by the intrepid duo of Taya Graham and Stephen Janis), and *The Chris Hedges Report*. And, during my two years at TRNN, we have built up a text publishing arm from scratch, which has enabled us to publish in-depth reporting and critical analysis by amazing authors such as Kim Kelly, Adam Johnson, Luis Feliz Leon, and more.

On top of directing, commissioning, editing, and shaping our content across the network, I also do a lot of reporting myself. I've covered many stories and big topics that are of interest to Real News audiences, but my main "beat" is labor. And while I considered talking today about the long death—and the recent, minor resurgence—of the labor beat, once a mainstay of nearly every newspaper in this country, I'm actually going to go in a different direction.[2]

Every week I conduct long-form, sprawling, even meandering interviews with workers of all stripes about their lives, jobs, dreams, and struggles—workers like Jonnie, a Delta flight attendant; Albert Elliott, a fired Amazon worker and organizer in North Carolina; Reagan, an exotic dancer in North Hollywood; Caleb and Andrew, two graduate student workers at Johns Hopkins University; Jay, a longtime railroad dispatcher; Arianna, a Starbucks worker in New York; and Leo, who was working on the *Deepwater Horizon* drilling rig on the day it blew up in 2010, killing eleven workers and causing the largest marine oil spill in human history.

When I say I'm uncomfortable calling this work journalism, that's not because I'm paying undue deference to the institution of Journalism with a capital "J" or that I'm being falsely modest about the value of conducting these kinds of interviews. Obviously, I think it's valuable, I wouldn't have devoted my life to it if I thought otherwise. However, I've been hesitant to call my approach journalistic from the moment I first started recording and publishing these interviews for my podcast *Working People* years ago to now also getting to do them for the Real News Network, for my guest segments at *Breaking Points*, and my book *The Work of Living*. To be blunt, I do not treat any conversational partner as a subject with a perspective on a larger story that I plan to balance out with differing perspectives and real-time fact-checking. As I tell every worker I talk to before we start recording, their life and their experience *is* the story. When you are talking to someone who is, as we all are, the foremost expert on their own experience, who the hell are you to fact-check their story? Of course, my conversational partner and I will provide as much factual context as we can for viewers and listeners if that story involves, for example, a union drive or instances of mistreatment, exploitation, and bullying. Although, ultimately, we are searching for something deeper than fact. As the great interviewer Studs Terkel once said, and I'm paraphrasing here, a person may not remember the fine lines and every minute detail when recounting a memory that is important to them—maybe the event they're recalling happened on a Wednesday, or maybe it was a Tuesday—but they still speak with indelible clarity the truth of their experience. Like Studs, I consider seeking out the truth my charge and vocation.

There's another reason I'm hesitant to call myself a journalist, which is painfully apparent to anyone who watches, reads, or listens to me for more than two seconds: I wear what colleagues in the media would call my "biases" on my sleeve. I get angry when workers tell me they are being exploited, I express my solidarity and support when they tell me about standing up for themselves and fighting for what they deserve. And when working people do stand up against unjust treatment, when they band together, when they refuse to believe they are as worthless and expendable as this system makes us out to be, and when they believe in themselves enough to try to change their given circumstances and struggle for a better life, *I want them to win.*

I don't know if that's journalism; however, I do know that if a free press is essential for the possibility of democratic society, but that press does not value the truth that makes society human as much as it values journalistic "objectivity" and impartial fact, it cannot deliver on its promise. The overwhelming absence of truthful reporting about the lives and experiences of everyday people, working people, the masses, the rank and file, the non-elites, and the rabble, is, I'd argue, one of the most pervasive and sinister forms of censorship. And what makes it so sinister is the fact that we have grown so accustomed to that absence that we hardly notice that anything's missing, nor do we feel like it is an antidemocratic, dehumanizing injustice that must be rectified. But it is.

It is not an accident that the ways we consume and share news today—and the ways news is packaged as something to be consumed and shared—are often directly at odds with our needs as engaged democratic citizens. Every day, with brutally dizzying speed, the content stream drags us along. As we struggle to keep our heads above water and stay informed about the world around us, the news from yesterday, from this morning, is already a distant, fading memory. But how has that information empowered us to act? What can we *do* with it? What else can we do besides consume it—or bite-sized versions of it—and move on, lest we drown in the flood that's always coming? In headlines, tweets, listicles, and snappy cable segments, the news is meant to command momentary attention and elicit a fleeting reaction, not to encourage deep thought or sustained empathy and emotional investment, and certainly not to foster any concerted action by working people to address the issues of the day. And we, in turn, have become the passive spectators and reliable consumers the news industry needs us to be to sustain its business model.

Here's the thing, though: "Staying informed" is not an end in itself. Informed for what? The democratic function and the civic necessity of a free press go far beyond informing people about the goings-on of their world: They are supposed to empower us to act more effectively in it, to provide the resources we need to be active shapers and stewards of democracy itself.

If nothing else, the state of our world today has demonstrated how dangerous and destructive it is to abandon the goal of maintaining an informed and democratically engaged public for the goal of creating a profitable and politically disengaged audience of consumers—and, as a result, leaving the questions of governance to be settled by powerful elites while the rest of us do nothing but watch the world burn through 3D glasses. Because watching is what we've been trained to do; it's all corporate-captured, profit-seeking, status-quo-fortifying media really allows us to do.

Nowhere is this more apparent than in the media's tacit and explicit complicity in creating and fortifying the capitalist fiction that democracy and work have nothing to do with each other. We spend most of our lives at work. The workplace is one of the most common and consequential venues of social and existential engineering. Yet our existence in the workplace is largely a blackhole of democratic being, a shared non-space where we are not only treated like subhuman organic machines with no democratic freedoms or, in many cases, even basic human rights. The workplace is also where we are conditioned, day by day, to believe that this is an unchangeable fact of life, like gravity, that we don't deserve anything better and do not have the power to do anything about it.

This is why I do what I do. This is why I focus on the stories and struggles of working people. It is important to make visible the raw, pulsing humanity that capitalist society tries so hard to render invisible; there is an urgent, moral, political, and, I would argue, civic need to make it impossible for people to ignore the whole human being behind every name tag, every job title, and every service that we depend on—because once you see that, you can't unsee it. Capitalism has essentially made it impossible for us to feel common humanity that we share with one another. But if we start to revivify those frayed nerve endings, if we start to reconnect with each other through the ties that bind us as fellow workers, citizens, and human beings, and if we learn to understand the backstories and yearnings and the livelihoods of people who provide the "essential labor" that we all depend on—and I don't mean that only in the terms by which the government defines "essential" labor—I mean parents, gig workers, sex workers, hospital workers, and everyone else who does the labor that keeps us and our world afloat. If we see the humanity behind all that labor, then we can feel the solidarity that the ruling class and the power-serving manufacturers of consent have tried to keep us from feeling for so long. And solidarity is the soil from which a new world, a better world for all of us, can grow. That is the truth you'll find in the kind of coverage that we try to do at the Real News Network.

It is the truth that reminds us that we are beautiful, that our lives are valuable, that we deserve to live with dignity, that we have rights, that things don't have to be this way, that they could be better, and that we have it within our power to make it so. The media's role in devaluing and erasing that truth has made it unforgivably complicit in the capitalistic scheme to make us into the disempowered, exploitable subjects that we are today. But we can change that.

MAXIMILLIAN ALVAREZ is editor-in-chief of The Real News Network, author of *The Work of Living: Working People Talk About Their Lives and the Year the World Broke*, and host of the *Working People* podcast.

Notes

1   *Editor's note*: This chapter is adapted from remarks delivered by the author for the keynote panel at the third annual Critical Media Literacy Conference of the Americas, held in Oakland, CA, October 21-23, 2022. Special thanks to Reagan Haynie, Project Censored's 2022-23 academic intern, for help with the transcription of Alvarez's remarks.
2   On the "long death" of the labor beat, see Christopher R. Martin, *No Longer Newsworthy: How the Mainstream Media Abandoned the Working Class* (Ithaca and London: ILR Press, 2019).

Acknowledgments

This book represents the commitment, coordination, and contributions of many people, not only those whose names are listed in its table of contents. We welcome the occasion to recognize many of them here.

Shealeigh Voitl edited *State of the Free Press 2024*. Her careful attention to detail and deep understanding of the Project and its mission is evident in subtle but significant ways on every page of this book.

Nora Barrows-Friedman, Mischa Geracoulis, Veronica Santiago Liu, T.M. Scruggs, and Dan Simon serve with us on the editorial board of the Censored Press. Now entering its fourth year of operation under this group's wise guidance, the Censored Press partners with Seven Stories Press to publish the Censored yearbook series and additional titles that promote political engagement informed by independent journalism and critical media literacy.

At Seven Stories Press, we thank Dan Simon, publisher and editorial director; Jon Gilbert, operations director; Ruth Weiner, publicity director and co-publisher of Triangle Square Books for Young Readers; Stewart Cauley, art director; Claire Kelley, marketing director; Tal Mancini, production editor; Bill Rusin, sales director; Allison Paller, web marketing manager; James Webster, social media; Anastasia Damaskou, publicist; Silvia Stramenga, foreign rights director; Eva Sotomayor, publicity; Catherine Taylor, SSP UK; Oona Holahan, and Noa Mendoza.

Anson Stevens-Bollen created original artwork for *State of the Free Press 2024*. His cover image provides an apt preview of the darker themes and sinister characters lurking within this year's book. We're honored and energized by our ongoing partnership with Anson, who also created the story icons that add visual vim to Chapter 1.

We are grateful for the extraordinary generosity of our donors, many of whom have supported us for years, including Steven Alexander, Cooper Atkinson, Heidi Boghosian, Sandra Cioppa, James Coleman, Jan De Deka, Dmitry Egerov, Larry Gassan, Martha Fleischman, Leonard C. Goodman, Michael Hansen, Leo Horrigan, William Kuendig, Sheldon Levy, James March, James McFadden, Harry Mersmann, David Nelson, Christopher Oscar, Aaron Placensia, Allison Reilly, Krista Rojas, John and Lyn Roth, T.M. Scruggs, David Stanek, Lana Touchstone, Sheila Weidenfeld, Michelle Westover, and Montgomery Zukowski.

We also thank the following institutions for essential support, including the Free Press, the Future of Life Foundation, the Silicon Valley Community Foundation, ISL Enterprises, and Peace Action Manhattan.

The Media Freedom Foundation's (MFF) board of directors, identified below, provides key counsel and support for our ongoing operations. Even in alleged retirement, MFF's emeritus president and co-founder, Peter Phillips, continues to bolster the Project's work and inspire our efforts on behalf of press freedoms and people-powered democracy.

Since 2006, Adam Armstrong has worked to ensure that Project Censored engages a global audience. Adam continues to serve as the Project's director of communications and outreach. As if that's not enough, he is also the

Media Freedom Foundation's CFO, keeping our budget in order and our financial books squeaky clean.

Lorna Garano of Lorna Garano Book Publicity amplifies the impact of Project Censored's work and expands our circle of allies. In a media ecosystem where everyone is clamoring for attention, Lorna assures that the Project's signal (including each of the titles published by the Censored Press) never gets lost in the noise.

We are grateful to Lyssa Schmidt and all at Presence & Company for grant writing support. Partnering with Lyssa and her team during the past year has challenged us to think in new ways about how to best represent the Project and its mission.

In 2022-23, student interns working with Project Censored played a vital role in our day-to-day operations, supporting the Project's work behind the scenes while also contributing to Project publications, social media, and radio programs. Warm thanks and best wishes to Kate Horgan, Annie Koruga, Sam Peacock, and Lauren Reduzzi (Summer 2022); Reagan Haynie (academic year 2022-23); and Riley Cummins, Grace Harty, Libby Meagher, and Ashton Sidford (Summer 2023) for their great work and good cheer.

The credibility of the Project hinges on the factual accuracy of its work. *State of the Free Press 2024* has benefited from careful fact-checking and proofreading by Riley Cummins, Reagan Haynie, Jen Lyons, Steve Macek, Libby Meagher, Ashton Sidford, and Shealeigh Voitl.

The Project Censored Show on Pacifica Radio, which originates from the historic studios of KPFA in Berkeley, California, continues to broadcast on more than fifty stations around the United States, from Maui to New York.

Special thanks to our senior producer and man behind the curtain, Anthony Fest; co-host and producer, Eleanor Goldfield; and KPFA event staff, including Kevin Hunsanger and Brandi Howell.

We are fortunate to work with wonderful people and organizations that not only share our mission to promote press freedoms but also help to spread the word about the Project's work, including Clayton Weimers of Reporters Without Borders; Maya Schenwar and Alana Yu-lan Price with Truthout; Heidi Boghosian and Marjorie Cohn of *Law and Disorder Radio*; Peter Maravelis, City Lights Foundation; Nolan Higdon, Allison Butler, and the organizing committee of the Critical Media Literacy Conference of the Americas; our friends and colleagues at the Union for Democratic Communications; Sonali Kolhatkar of *Rising Up With Sonali*; Michael Welch of *Global Research News Hour*; Geoffrey Riley, Angela Decker, and Nash Bennett of the *Jefferson Exchange*; Garland Nixon, host of *NewsViews*; Deb Hobson, host of *Chautauqua* on KOPN; Lee Camp, host of *Moment of Clarity*; Mitch Ratcliffe, host of the *Earth911* podcast; Nicole Sandler of the *Nicole Sandler Show*; Joe Richey of *Hemispheres* (KGNU); Nancy Price, Jim Tarbell, and colleagues at the Alliance for Democracy; Annie Esposito and Steve Scalmanini, cohosts of *Corporations and Democracy* (KZYX); Lynn Feinerman at *Women Rising Radio*; Jeff Share and colleagues with the UNESCO DCMÉT International Symposium on Democracy, Global Citizenship, and Transformative Education; Joe Aguiar, Dan Newmyer, and Barth Keck of *CT Politics*; Karen Hunter of the *Karen Hunter Show*; Roy Ice, William Schloetel, and the team at *Lifestyle Magazine*; Ralph Nader of the *Ralph Nader Radio*

Hour, Chris Hedges of the *Chris Hedges Report*; David Feldman of the *David Feldman Show*; Sharyl Attkisson of *Full Measure with Sharyl Attkisson*; *MintCast* with Mnar Adley and Alan MacLeod; Eric Draitser, Jeffrey St. Clair, and the crew at *CounterPunch*; Mitch Jeserich, host of *Letters and Politics* on Pacifica Radio; Davey D and all at *Hard Knock Radio*; Abby Martin of the *Empire Files*; Tracy Rosenberg of Media Alliance; Stephen Jay and Jeff Van Treese of *Mobilized* on Free Speech TV; *The Zero Hour* with RJ Eskow; *Parallax Views* with J.G. Michael; *Tell Me Everything* with John Fugelsang; Max Tegmark and the team at Improve the News; Chase Palmieri at Credder; Angie Tibbs and the team at Dissident Voice; The Avid Reader bookstore in Sacramento; the Sebastiani Theater in Sonoma, CA; Medea Benjamin and all at CodePink; Evelyn McDonnell and Kyra Pearson at Loyola Marymount University in Los Angeles; Sheri Whalen and Andy Duncan at Frostburg State University in Maryland; James Preston Allen and the staff at *Random Lengths News*; the Association of Alternative Newsmedia (AAN); Page Against the Machine bookstore in Long Beach, CA; Sydney Sullivan at UC Davis; Daniel Faulkenberry, who teaches in the Natomas Unified School District; Kevin Gosztola of Shadowproof, who hosts the *Unauthorized Disclosure* podcast; Maximillian Alvarez and all our allies at the Real News Network; Raza Rumi at Ithaca College's Park Center for Independent Media; John Collins, Jana Morgan, Cecilia Hyland, and the entire Weave News crew; Julian Vigo at Savage Minds; Robert Scheer and the ScheerPost team; the Independent Media Institute; *Ms. Magazine*; Salon; *YES! Magazine*; *The Progressive*, with thanks to Norman Stockwell; Chris Finan and all at the National Coalition Against Censorship; and Betsy Gomez and the Banned Books Week Coalition.

At Diablo Valley College, Mickey thanks Obed Vazquez, Dean of Social Science; Lisa Martin, John Corbally, Carmina Quirarte, Matthew Powell, Nolan Higdon, Michael Levitin, Rosa Del Duca, Charleen Earley, Donna Smith, John Kropf, Adam Bessie, Rayshell Clapper, Andrea Sorce, Robert Abele, and Jacob van Vleet; in the Social Justice Studies program, Sangha Niyogi and Albert Ponce; John Freytag and Lisa Smiley-Ratchford of the Academic Senate; Beth Arman, Dean of Career and Community Partnership; Doug Phenix, Demetria Lawrence, Vice President Joe Gorga, and President Susan Lamb, as well as all of the students from this past year who came back to campus. It is an honor to be back in the classroom with each of them!

Mickey especially thanks his wife Meg and their two children for their ongoing love, patience, and support, as without them this work would not be possible. Andy is grateful for Elizabeth Boyd's steadfast support and good humor, as well as the loving care of his parents and extended family.

And, finally, thanks to you, our readers, for the ongoing uplift, which inspires and enhances the Project's work to promote press freedom, media literacy, and informed civic engagement.

MEDIA FREEDOM FOUNDATION/PROJECT CENSORED BOARD OF DIRECTORS

Adam Armstrong, Ben Boyington, Kenn Burrows, Allison Butler (vice president), Eleanor Goldfield, Doug Hecker,

Mickey Huff (president), Veronica Santiago Liu, Christopher Oscar, Andy Lee Roth, and T.M. Scruggs.

PROJECT CENSORED 2022-23 JUDGES

ROBIN ANDERSEN. Writer, commentator, and award-winning author. Professor Emerita of Communication and Media Studies at Fordham University. She edits the Routledge Focus Book Series on Media and Humanitarian Action. Her forthcoming books are *Death in Paradise: A Critical Study of the BBC Series* and *Censorship, Digital Media, and the Global Crackdown on Freedom of Expression*. She writes regularly for Fairness & Accuracy in Reporting (FAIR).

AVRAM ANDERSON. Collection Management Librarian, California State University, Northridge. A member and advocate of the LGBTQI+ community researching LGBTQ bias and censorship. Co-author of *The Media and Me: A Guide to Critical Media Literacy for Young People* (2022) and "Censorship by Proxy and Moral Panics in the Digital Era," in *Censorship, Digital Media, and the Global Crackdown on Freedom of Expression* (forthcoming). They also contribute to the *Index on Censorship*, *In These Times*, and Truthout.

HEIDI BOGHOSIAN. Attorney and activist. Author of *Spying on Democracy* (2013) and *I Have Nothing to Hide: And 20 Other Myths About Surveillance and Privacy* (2021), as well as several articles on the policing of First Amendment-protected activities. Co-host of *Law & Disorder Radio*.

KENN BURROWS. Teacher of Holistic Health Studies at San Francisco State University since 1991. Founder and Director of SFSU's Holistic Health Learning Center, an award-winning interdisciplinary library and community center. Since 2001, under his direction, the Center has hosted a biennial conference, "The Future of Healthcare," and annual educational events including Food Awareness Month and the Gandhi-King

Season for Nonviolence, an eighty-day educational campaign demonstrating how nonviolence empowers our personal and collective lives.

BRIAN COVERT. Journalist, author, and educator based in Japan. Worked for United Press International (UPI) news service in Japan, as a staff reporter and editor for English-language daily newspapers in Japan, and as contributing writer to Japanese and overseas newspapers and magazines. Contributing author to past editions of the *Censored* yearbook series. Teaches journalism at Doshisha University in Kyoto.

GEOFF DAVIDIAN. Investigative reporter, publisher, editor, war correspondent, and educator. He has taught journalism in the US, UK, and India and reported on international terrorism, Middle Eastern affairs, Congress, local government corruption, and breaches of legal and judicial ethics, for which he twice received the Gavel Award from the State Bar of Texas. Founding publisher and editor of the *Putnam Pit*.

MISCHA GERACOULIS. Journalist and contributing editor at *The Markaz Review* and editorial board member at the Censored Press. Research concentrated on the intersections among critical media and information literacy, human rights education, democracy, and ethics. Priority issues include truth in reporting, press and academic freedoms, the protracted disinformation campaign against the Armenian Genocide, and diasporic identities and cultures.

ROBERT HACKETT. Professor Emeritus of Communication, Simon Fraser University, Vancouver. Co-founder of NewsWatch Canada (1993), Media Democracy Days (2001), and OpenMedia.ca (2007). His eight books on media and politics include *Journalism and Climate Crisis: Public Engagement, Media Alternatives* (with S. Forde, S. Gunster, and K. Foxwell-Norton, 2017) and *Remaking Media: The Struggle to Democratize Public Communication* (with W.K. Carroll, 2006). Winner of the 2018

SFU Award for community impact. He writes for thetyee.ca, nationalobserver.com, rabble.ca, and other media.

KEVIN HOWLEY. Professor of Media Studies at DePauw University. Before joining academia, he worked in community media as a trainer and producer. In addition to his record of peer-reviewed scholarly publication, he has worked as a newspaper columnist, radio broadcaster, and video producer. His current research and teaching interests include participatory media, multimodal writing, and critical utopianism.

NICHOLAS JOHNSON.* Author, *How to Talk Back to Your Television Set* (1970) and nine more books, including *Columns of Democracy* (2018) and *What Do You Mean and How Do You Know?* (2009). Commissioner, Federal Communications Commission (1966–1973); Professor, University of Iowa College of Law (1981–2014, media law and cyber law). More at nicholasjohnson.org.

CHARLES L. KLOTZER. Founder, editor, and publisher emeritus of *St. Louis Journalism Review* and *FOCUS/Midwest*. The *St. Louis Journalism Review* has been transferred to Southern Illinois University, Carbondale, and is now the *Gateway Journalism Review*. Klotzer remains active at the *Review*.

NANCY KRANICH. Teaching Professor, School of Communication and Information, and special projects librarian, Rutgers University. Past president of the American Library Association (ALA), member of ALA's Freedom to Read Foundation Roll of Honor, and convener of the ALA Center for Civic Life. Author of hundreds of publications, including *Libraries and Democracy: The Cornerstones of Liberty* (2001), "Adventures in Information Policy Wonderland" (2019), and "Libraries: Reuniting the Divided States of America" (2017).

MARTIN LEE. Investigative journalist and author. Co-founder of Fairness & Accuracy In Reporting and former editor of FAIR's magazine, *Extra!* Director of Project CBD, a medical science information nonprofit. Author of *Smoke Signals: A Social History of Marijuana—Medical, Recreational, and Scientific* (2012); *The Beast Reawakens: Fascism's Resurgence from Hitler's Spymasters to Today's Neo-Nazi Groups and Right-Wing Extremists* (2000); and *Acid Dreams: The Complete Social History of LSD: The CIA, the Sixties, and Beyond* (with B. Shlain, 1985).

PETER LUDES. Visiting Positions in Sociology at the Universities of Newfoundland and Amsterdam; Professor of Culture and Media Science at the University of Siegen (Germany); Visiting Positions at Harvard, Mannheim, and Constance; and Visiting Research Professor in Comparative Cultures at the University of Cologne, since 2018. Professor of Mass Communication, Jacobs University, Bremen, 2002–2017. Founder of the German Initiative on News Enlightenment (1997) at the University of Siegen. Recent publications on brutalization and banalization (2018) and collective myths and decivilizing processes (with Stefan Kramer, 2020).

DANIEL MÜLLER. Head of the Postgraduate Academy at the University of Siegen, in Germany. Researcher and educator in journalism, mass communication studies, and history at public universities for many years. Has published extensively on media history, media–minority relations in Germany, and nationality policies and ethnic relations of the Soviet Union and the post-Soviet successor states, particularly in the Caucasus. Jury member of the German Initiative on News Enlightenment.

JACK L. NELSON.* Distinguished Professor Emeritus, Graduate School of Education, Rutgers University. Former member, Committee on Academic Freedom and Tenure, American Association of University Professors. Recipient, Academic Freedom Award, National Council for Social Studies. Author of seventeen books, including *Critical Issues in Education: Dialogues and Dialectics*, 9th ed. (with S. Palonsky and M.R. McCarthy,

2021) and *Human Impact of Natural Disasters* (with V.O. Pang and W.R. Fernekes, 2010), and about two hundred articles.

PETER PHILLIPS. Professor Emeritus of Political Sociology, Sonoma State University. Director, Project Censored, 1996–2010. President, Media Freedom Foundation, 2010–2016. Editor or co-editor of fourteen editions of the *Censored* yearbook series. Author of *Giants: The Global Power Elite* (2018). Co-editor (with Dennis Loo) of *Impeach the President: The Case Against Bush and Cheney* (2006).

MICHAEL RAVNITZKY. Attorney, writer, editor, engineer, and Freedom of Information Act expert who has developed tools to broaden access to public records in the public interest.

T.M. SCRUGGS. Professor Emeritus (token ethnomusicologist), University of Iowa. Print, audio, and/or video format publications on media in Nicaragua and Venezuela, as well as on Central American, Cuban, Venezuelan, and US music and dance. Involvement with community radio in Nicaragua, Venezuela, and the United States, including the KPFA (Berkeley, CA) Local Station Board and Pacifica National Board. Executive producer, *The Nine Lives of Barbara Dane* and other documentaries. Board member, The Real News Network and Truthout.

PAUL STREET. Researcher, award-winning journalist, historian, author, and speaker. Author of ten books to date: *This Happened Here: Neoliberals, Amerikaners, and the Trumping of America* (Routledge, October 2021); *Hollow Resistance: Obama, Trump and the Politics of Appeasement* (CounterPunch, 2020); *They Rule: The 1% vs. Democracy* (2014); *Crashing the Tea Party* (with Anthony R. DiMaggio, 2011); *The Empire's New Clothes* (2010); *Barack Obama and the Future of American Politics* (2009); *Racial Oppression in the Global Metropolis* (2007); *Still Separate, Unequal* (2005); *Segregated Schools: Educational Apartheid in Post–Civil Rights America* (2005); and *Empire and Inequality* (2004). He writes regularly for *CounterPunch*.

SHEILA RABB WEIDENFELD.* Emmy Award-winning television producer. Former press secretary to Betty Ford and special assistant to the President; author, *First Lady's Lady*. President of DC Productions Ltd. Creator of snippetsofwisdom.com. Director of community relations of Phyto Management LLC and Maryland Cultivation and Processing LLC.

ROB WILLIAMS. Founding president of the Action Coalition for Media Education (ACME). Teaches media, communications, global studies, and journalism at Champlain and Saint Michael's Colleges and Northern Vermont University. Author of numerous articles on critical media literacy education. Publisher of the *Vermont Independent* online news journal. Author of *The Post (Truth) World* (2019) and *Media Mojo!* (2020), and co-editor of *Media Education for a Digital Generation* (with J. Frechette, 2016) and *Most Likely to Secede* (with R. Miller, 2013), about the Vermont independence movement.

*Indicates having been a Project Censored judge since our founding in 1976.

How To Support Project Censored

NOMINATE A STORY

To nominate a *Censored* story, forward the URL to andy@projectcensored.org. The deadline to nominate stories for the next yearbook is March 31, 2024.

Criteria for Project Censored story nominations:

1) A censored news story reports information that the public has a right and a need to know, but to which the public has had limited access.
2) The news story is recent, having been first reported no later than one year ago. Stories submitted for *State of the Free Press 2025* should be no older than April 2023.
3) The story is fact-based with clearly defined concepts and verifiable documentation. The story's claims should be supported by evidence—the more controversial the claims, the stronger the evidence necessary.
4) The news story has been published, either electronically or in print, in a publicly circulated newspaper, journal, magazine, newsletter, or similar publication from a journalistic source.

MAKE A TAX-DEDUCTIBLE DONATION

We depend on tax-deductible donations to continue our work. Project Censored is supported by the Media Freedom Foundation, a 501(c)(3) nonprofit organization. To support our efforts on behalf of independent journalism and freedom of information, send checks to the address below or donate online at projectcensored.org. Your generous donations help us to oppose news censorship and promote media literacy.

Media Freedom Foundation
PO Box 1177
Fair Oaks, CA 95628

About the Editors

ANDY LEE ROTH is the associate director of Project Censored and co-editor of fourteen editions of the Project's yearbook. He helps coordinate the Project's Campus Affiliates Program, a news media research network of several hundred students and faculty at two dozen colleges and universities across North America. In addition to co-authoring *The Media and Me*, Project Censored's guide to critical media literacy for young people, Roth has published research and articles in the *Index on Censorship*; *In These Times*; *YES! Magazine*; Truthout; *Media, Culture & Society*; the *International Journal of Press/Politics*; and other outlets. He earned a PhD in sociology at the University of California, Los Angeles, and a BA in sociology and anthropology at Haverford College. He lives in Winthrop, Washington, with his sweetheart.

MICKEY HUFF is the director of Project Censored and president of the nonprofit Media Freedom Foundation. To date, he has coedited fifteen editions of the Project's yearbook. He is also the co-author, with Nolan Higdon, of *Let's Agree to Disagree* (Routledge, 2022), a practical handbook on critical thinking and civil discourse, and *United States of Distraction* (City Lights, 2019); and a co-author of *The Media and Me: A Guide to Critical Media Literacy for Young People*. Huff is a professor of social science, history, and journalism at Diablo Valley College, where he co-chairs the History Area and is chair of the Journalism

Department. In 2019, he received the Beverly Kees Educator Award from the Society of Professional Journalists' Northern California chapter. Huff is co-host and executive producer of *The Project Censored Show*, the Project's syndicated public affairs radio program. A musician and composer, he lives with his family in Fair Oaks, California.

For more information about the editors, to invite them to speak at your school or in your community, or to conduct interviews, please visit projectcensored.org/press-room.

Index

E

East Palestine, Ohio, 80, 81, 135, 158, *see also* Ohio train derailment

Eat This, Not That! (media franchise), 85-86

eclampsia, 49

Economic Policy Institute, 55, 56, 57

Economic Roundtable (public policy organization), 83

economics, *see* employment, inflation, labor

The Economist, 76

Edison Electric Institute, 65

education, 75, 123-24, *see also* book bans, critical media literacy, "informal removal" policies

colleges and universities, 17, 60-62, 93-94, 95-96

parents' rights, 189

public, 182

Ehrler, Abby, 111

elections, 121, 123-4, 153-5, 194, 197

Electric Power Research Institute, 65

electric utilities, 17, 65-67, 70-71

Elizabeth Taylor AIDS Foundation, 92

Elk, Mike, 41

Elliott, Albert, 206

Ellis, Christina, 191

Ellsberg, Daniel, vii, 179-80, 182-3

Emeran, Christine, 10, 182, 188-92

employment, 17, 82-83

Energy Charter Treaty (ECT), 46-47

Engel, Grace, 48

environmental activism, *see* activism

Environmental Protection Agency (EPA) (US), 24-25, 30-33, 81, 158

Environmental Health Perspectives, 50

Environmental Research Letters, 65-67

Environmental Science & Technology, 23

Epstein, Jeffrey, 170

Equatorial Guinea, 95

Erdogan, Recep, 187

Escazú Agreement, 53

Espionage Act of 1917 (US), 164, 181, 199

Essence (magazine), 67, 68

ETH Zurich (university), 23, 25

European Union (EU), 32, 47, 167

Everytown for Gun Safety, 77-79

Extra! (Fairness and Accuracy in Reporting), 106, 107

ExxonMobil, 56, 61, 67, 69, 71

⌈CP⌉ THE CENSORED PRESS

The Censored Press is the publishing imprint of Project Censored and its nonprofit sponsor, the Media Freedom Foundation. Building on the Project's yearbook series, website, weekly radio show, and other educational programs, the Censored Press advances the Project's mission to promote independent investigative journalism, media literacy, and critical thinking.

The Censored Press benefits from a robust partnership with Seven Stories Press, the Project's longtime publisher and stalwart ally, which prints and distributes Censored Press titles.

To date, the Censored Press has published *The Media and Me: A Guide to Critical Media Literacy for Young People*, by Project Censored and the Media Revolution Collective (2022); Kevin Gosztola's *Guilty of Journalism: The Political Case Against Julian Assange* (2023); Adam Bessie and Peter Glanting's *Going Remote: A Teacher's Journey* (2023); and the three most recent volumes of Project Censored's *State of the Free Press* yearbook series. Forthcoming titles include Peter Phillips' *Titans of Capital*, which updates and expands his 2018 book, *Giants: The Global Power Elite*, and Omar Zahzah's *Terms of Servitude: Zionism, Silicon Valley, and Digital Colonialism in the Palestinian Liberation Struggle*.

The generosity of several founding donors ensures that the Censored Press will be a sustainable publishing imprint, but generous support from new donors expands our capacity to produce additional titles and provide new opportunities for reporting, teaching, and thinking critically.

https://censoredpress.org/